I Do, I Do

American Wedding Etiquette of Yesteryear

I Do, I Do

American Wedding Etiquette of Yesteryear

EDITED BY

SUSANNAH A. DRIVER

Hippocrene Books, Inc.
New York

ISBN 0-7818-0650-X

For information, address:
HIPPOCRENE BOOKS, INC.
171 Madison Avenue
New York, NY 10016

Printed in the United States of America

Contents

ॐ

Preface

"Manners are the happy way of doing things."
—Ralph Waldo Emerson

Whenever there's a wedding to go to or plan, questions of good manners and correct behavior inevitably arise. This was all the more true for brides and grooms and their families, attendants, and invited guests in the last two decades of the nineteenth century and the first three of our own.

They were decades of great changes in fashion, as well as in many social mores, including roles for women and relations between the sexes. All of which had an effect on how, or whether, to properly carry out the seemingly timeless traditions one felt a wedding ought to embody, while also being absolutely up to date with current manners.

How many bridesmaids should one have? What time of day is appropriate for the ceremony? What happens at a formal wedding versus an informal one? Is a wedding ring required? What will one say on the receiving line? Where should one seat the groom's parents at the reception? How many tea towels were *really* necessary in one's trousseau? Fortunately, there were etiquette authorities to help one sort it all out, and whose books now give us an enlightening and entertaining glimpse at how earlier Americans conducted themselves (or were meant to) and at the background of many customs practiced today. This is a look at a set that thought of itself "polite society" and "the great world," that prided itself on being and looking "smart" and doing things according to "Good Form." They were at least comfortable, and some were fabulously wealthy. Most were Protestant and of European background.

Then as now, many years of precedent had handed down guidelines on every detail from the order of the service to the placement of the guests and the music all would hear. Yet each period has its own variations on the theme. Many of the customs of "polite society" are familiar today, though in modified form. Others may seem like quaint artifacts of an era that has forever vanished. Through the ways that world married its own we can glimpse a way of life that is no more, and yet lives on in contemporary interpretations of all the practices that surround the saying of "I do."

CHAPTER 1

The Engagement

COURTSHIP

Choosing one's life partner has always been a weighty step. It was a matter not beneath the serious attention of our own first president, and as late as 1879, the advice of George Washington was still considered useful to women contemplating matrimony. His letter outlining a few basic principles and cautions were reprinted in a guide to etiquette of the day, and it no doubt still speaks to those of a mind to get engaged:

Gen'l George Washington's Letter of Advice to Miss Nellie Custis in the Selecting of a Husband.

MEN and women, feel the same inclination towards each other now that they always have done, and which they will continue to do, until there is a new order of things; and you, as others have done, may find that the passions of your sex are easier raised than allayed. Do not, therefore, boast too soon, nor too strongly of your insensibility. ° ° ° Love is said to be an involuntary passion, and it is, therefore, contended that it cannot be resisted. This is true in part only, for like all things

else, when nourished and supplied plentifully with aliment, it is rapid in its progress; but let these be withdrawn, and it may be stifled in its growth. Although we cannot avoid first impressions, we may assuredly place them under guard. ❋ ❋ ❋ When the fire is beginning to kindle and your heart growing warm, propound these questions to it. Who is the invader? Have I a competent knowledge of him? Is he a man of good character? A man of sense? For, be assured, a sensible woman can never be happy with a fool. What has been his walk in life? ❋ ❋ ❋ Is his fortune sufficient to maintain me in the manner I have been accustomed to live, and as my sisters do live? And is he one to whom my friends can have no reasonable objection? If all these interrogatories can be satisfactorily answered, there will remain but one more to be asked; that, however, is an important one. Have I sufficient ground to conclude that his affections are engaged by me? Without this the heart of sensibility will struggle against a passion that is not reciprocated.

Yours affectionately,
GEORGE WASHINGTON.

— *Wedding Etiquette and Usages of Polite Society*

Not only was a young woman to be careful about who she chose; she was to be very careful about the company she kept, and where and when she did what with whom, while going about meeting prospective husbands. Fortunately, in the process of courtship a young woman of the 1920s could rely on extensive, detailed advice from a new source — Emily Post (née Price), who came out with the first edition of her now classic *Etiquette: The Blue Book of Social Usage* in 1922.

In order to conduct a blameless courtship, a woman needed to know the rules governing what circumstances require a chaperon and which kinds of people make acceptable chaperons. Then, she can experience the:

Freedom of the Chaperoned

As a matter of fact the only young girl who is really "free," is she whose chaperon is never very far away. She need give conventionality very little thought, and not bother about her P's and Q's at all, because her chaperon is always a strong and protective defense; but a young girl who is unprotected by a chaperon is in the position precisely of an unarmed traveler walking alone among wolves—his only defense is in not attracting their notice.

To be sure the time has gone by when an elderly lady is indispensable to every gathering of young people. Young girls for whose sole benefit and protection the chaperon exists (she does not exist for her own pleasure, youthful opinion to the contrary notwithstanding), have infinitely greater freedom from her surveillance than had those of other days, and the typical chaperon is seldom seen with any but very young girls, too young to have married friends. Otherwise a young married woman, bride perhaps scarcely out of her teens, is, on all ordinary occasions, a perfectly suitable chaperon, especially if her husband is present. A very young married woman gadding about without her husband is not a proper chaperon.

There are also many occasions when a chaperon is unnecessary! It is considered perfectly correct for a young girl to drive a motor by herself, or take a young man with her, if her family know and approve of him, for any short distance in the country. She may play golf, tennis, go to the Country Club, or Golf Club (if near by), sit on the beach, go canoeing, ride horseback, and take part in the normal sports and occupations of country life. Young girls always go to private parties of every sort without their own chaperon, but the fact that a lady issues an invitation means that either she or another suitable chaperon will be present.

—Etiquette

To choose the person who can give courting woman this delicious freedom, the following should be kept in mind:

IT goes without saying that a chaperon is always a lady, often one whose social position is better than that of her charge; occasionally, she is a social sponsor as well as a moral one. Her position, if she is not a relative, is very like that of a companion. Above all, a chaperon must have dignity, and if she is to be of any actual service, she must be kind of heart and have intelligent sympathy and tact. To have her charge not only care for her, but be happy with her, is the only possible way such a relationship can endure.

Needless to say a chaperon's own conduct must be irreproachable and her knowledge of the world such as can only be gained by personal experience; but she need not be an old lady! She can perfectly well be reasonably young, and a spinster.

Very often the chaperon "keeps the house," but she is never called a "housekeeper." Nor is she a "secretary" though she probably draws the checks and audits the bills.

It is by no means unusual for mothers who are either very gay or otherwise busy, and cannot give most of their time to their grown and growing daughters, to put them in charge of a resident chaperon. Often their governess— if she is a woman of the world—gives up her autocracy of the schoolroom and becomes social guardian instead.

ﬀﬁ ﬀﬁ ﬀﬁ

AT a dinner party given for young people in a private house, a somewhat older sister would be a sufficient chaperon. Or the young hostess' mother after receiving the guests may, if she chooses, dine with her mother elsewhere than in the dining-room, the parents' roof being supposedly chaperonage enough.

In going to tea in a college man's room, or in a bachelor's apartment, the proper chaperon should be a lady of

fairly mature years. To see two or three apparently young people going into a bachelor's quarters would be open to criticism. There are many places which are unsuitable for young girls to go to whether they are chaperoned or not. No well brought up young girl should be allowed to go to supper at a cabaret until she is married, or has passed the age when "very young" can be applied to her.

—*Etiquette*

And although the word *chaperon*, even then, conjured "a humorless tyrant whose 'correct' manner plainly reveals her true purpose, which is to take the joy out of life," according to Emily Post "she can be—and often is—a perfectly human and sympathetic person, whose unselfish desire is merely to smooth the path of one who is the darling of her heart."

In what situations must this paragon have been present?

IT is not considered proper for a young girl ever to be alone as hostess. When she invites young girls and men to her house, Miss Titherington either "receives" them or comes into the room while they are there. If the time is afternoon, very likely she pours tea and when everyone has been helped, she goes into another room. She does not stay with them ever, but she is never very far away.

The chaperon (or a parent) should never go to bed until the last young man has left the house. It is an unforgivable breach of decorum to allow a young girl to sit up late at night with a young man—or a number of them. On returning home from a party, she must not invite or allow a man to "come in for a while." Even her fiancé must bid her good night at the door if the hour is late, and someone ought always to sit up, or get up, to let her in. No young girl ought to let herself in with a latch-key.

ʚ ʚ ʚ

A YOUNG girl may not, even with her fiancé, lunch in a road house without a chaperon, or go on a journey that can by any possibility last overnight. To go out with him in a small sail-boat sounds harmless enough, but might result in a questionable situation if they are becalmed, or if they are left helpless in a sudden fog. The Maine coast, for example, is particularly subject to fogs that often shut down without warning and no one going out on the water can tell whether he will be able to get back within a reasonable time or not. A man and a girl went out from Bar Harbor and did not get back until the next day. Everyone knew the fog had come in as thick as pea soup and that it was impossible to get home; but to the end of time her reputation will suffer for the experience.

—Etiquette

And as if these rules weren't enough, one had to recall that

Conventions . . . Change with Locality

IN New York, for instance, no young girl of social standing may, without being criticized, go alone with a man to the theater. Absolutely no lady (unless middle-aged—and even then she would be defying convention) can go to dinner or supper in a restaurant alone with a gentleman. A lady, not young, who is staying in a very dignified hotel, can have a gentleman dine with her. But nay married woman, if her husband does not object, may dine alone in her own home with any man she pleases or have a different one come in to tea every day in the week without being criticized.

A very young girl may motor around the country alone with a man, with her father's consent, or sit with him on the rocks by the sea or on a log in the woods; but she must not sit with him in a restaurant. All of which is about as upside down as it can very well be. In a restaurant they

are not only under the surveillance of many eyes, but they can scarcely speak without being over heard, whereas short-distance motoring, driving, riding, walking or sitting on the seashore has no element of protection certainly. Again, though she may not lunch with him in a restaurant, she is sometimes (not always) allowed to go to a moving picture matinée with him! Why sitting in the dark in a moving theater is allowed, and the restaurant is tabu is very mysterious.

Older girls and young married women are beginning to lunch with men they know well in some of the New York restaurants, but not in others. In many cities it would be scandalous for a young married woman to lunch with a man not her husband, but quite all right for a young girl and man to lunch at a country club. This last is reasonable because the room is undoubtedly filled with people they know — who act as potential chaperons. Nearly everywhere it is thought proper for them to go to a dancing club for tea, if the "club" is managed by a chaperon.

As said above, interpretation of what is proper shifts according to locality. Even in Victorian days it was proper in Baltimore for a young girl to go to the theater alone with a man, and to have him see her home from a ball was not only permitted but absolutely correct.

—Etiquette

An unmarried man who wished to invite his intended, or his hoped-for, to his home had to keep certain rules in mind as well.

IT is unnecessary to say no lady may dine alone in a gentleman's rooms, or house; nor may she dine with a number of gentlemen (unless one of them is her husband, in which case she is scarcely "alone"). But it is perfectly correct for two or more ladies to dine at a gentleman's rooms if one of the ladies is elderly or the husband of one is present.

A bachelor entertaining in bachelor's quarters, meaning that he has only a man servant, must be much more punctilious, and must arrange to have the chaperon bring any young woman guests with her, since no young girls could be seen entering bachelor's quarters alone, and have their "good name" survive. If he has a large establishment, including women servants, and if furthermore he is a man whose own reputation is unblemished, the chaperon may be met at his house. But since it is more prudent for young women to arrive under her care, why run the unnecessary risk of meeting Mrs. Grundy's jackal on the doorstep?

At the house of a bachelor such as described above, the chaperon could be a husbandless young married woman, or in other words, the most careless chaperon possible, without ever giving Mrs. Grundy's magpie cause for ruffling a feather. But no young woman could dine or have tea, no matter how well chaperoned, in the "rooms" of a man of morally bad reputation without running a very unpleasant risk of censure.

—Etiquette

THE PROPOSAL

Once the courtship was successfully accomplished, a man of the 1880s might avail himself of these sweet verses in proposing eternal union to his beloved.

If Thou'lt Be Mine.

"IF thou'lt be mine, the treasures of air,
    Of earth, and sea, shall lie at thy feet;
Whatever in Fancy's eye looks fair,
    Or in Hope's sweet music sounds most sweet,
    Shall be ours—if thou wilt be mine, love!"

"Bright flowers shall bloom wherever we rove,
  A voice divine shall talk in each stream;
The stars shall look like worlds of love,
  And this Earth be all one beautiful dream
  In our eyes—if thou wilt be mind, love!"
                              —*Thomas Moore.*

ℬ ℬ ℬ

From This Hour.

"FROM this hour, the pledge is given,
From this hour my soul is thine:
Come what will, from earth or heaven,
Weal or woe, thy fate is mine."
                              —*Thomas Moore.*

—*Wedding Etiquette and Usages of Polite Society*

At the same time, however, the business of engagement was not always seen so romantically:

THERE are certain subjects about which both men and women seem to think themselves privileged to be untruthful, and they are not slow to exercise the privilege. One of the subjects, with men, is business, and what belongs to it, such as capital, credit, profits. The topic that women are most prone to exercise their fancy on, irrespective of any basis of fact, is proposals of marriage, which they may regard as their business, since, unhappily, most women, when young, have no other business worthy the name. Their highest intelligence, their greatest energy, their best thought, is devoted to wedlock. They are taught to believe that wedlock is their destiny, and it must be conceded that, as a rule, they take no pains to counteract it. Naturally, they want to make the best match they can. They hope to love their husband; but they wish, very

reasonably, to have something besides their heart to support love.

Marriage is to them an ideal state, a husband is an ideal creature, until they have been attained. They think that they can secure the most desirable husbands by making themselves appear in active demand, which, connubially not less than commercially, enhance the price of the thing in the market. Every time that they have an offer, and the offer is made known, their chances for a marital prize are bettered; and every woman, whatever her lack of endowment, has at least a latent hope of winning a prize. If they do not have as many offers as they believe they ought to have, why should they not imagine or invent some? This is the suggestion of their vanity—the most dangerous tempter to a woman—and the suggestion once made cannot be forgotten. It is likely that the suggestion may not come in so definite a shape. The wish to be sought as a wife being so strong in the feminine breast, may it not become the father of the belief? May not women deceive themselves into thinking that men have proposed who have never dreamed of proposing? May they not see what they want to see? May they not hear what they want to hear?

This is true of some women, probably, but the mass of them undoubtedly stretch their conscience and the truth when they speak of their offers. The fact that any woman will or can make such a revelation, except under most extraordinary circumstances, is sufficient ground to discredit her. She who has the largest number of offers is apt to be she who is absolutely silent on that point. Men, however foolish in matters matrimonial—and they are as foolish as their worst enemy could ask—show a degree of discretion in committing themselves to women manifestly without reserve. Still, it is surprising and painful to think how many women of the better sort, women ordinarily possessed of delicacy, refinement, and trustworthiness, will deliberately falsify concerning the conduct of men they are or have been on terms with.

— Wedding Etiquette and Usages of Polite Society

But leave it to *Punch* to see the humor in the combination of romantic love and business arrangement that has been marriage for so many centuries:

A Proposal of the Period.

"I've rank and wealth; and, lady, here's my hand;
And never from you shall my fancy range."
"Yes; that's an offer I can understand:
But what am I to give you in exchange?"

"Well, in return I ask your heart." "Ah me!
Kind sir, I now must own my helplessness.
Ask me for anything but that. You see,
It's just the one thing that I don't possess."
—From *Punch*.

—Wedding Etiquette and Usages of Polite Society

Once all was settled between the two most concerned,

The Engagement.

THE engagement and its announcement, which is the first positive step towards marriage, is generally made known by the parties interested, each making the Engagement known to their special friends. It is the German custom to publish in the newspapers an engagement, same as we do marriages. When the Engagement is made public, the lady does not pay visits, except to her intimate friends; she leaves her visiting cards at her friends' residences just previous to the sending of her wedding invitations, which are sent at least two weeks previous to the occasion.

—Wedding Etiquette and Usages of Polite Society

By the 1890s, announcing the engagement was a more formal procedure, and the bride-to-be's parents may have had a more prominent role:

> THERE are various methods that good form approves for making marriage engagements known to the world. Sometimes the *fiancée's* family gives a dinner party to intimate friends, and the engagement is announced at table, after the dessert is removed. Sometimes an invitation mentions that the occasion is to celebrate a daughter's betrothal to Mr.———(the person's christian name is mentioned).
>
> If a girl has her bridesmaids already in mind, she writes notes to them, announcing her expectations, and she does the same to very near and dear elderly friends, because this method of communicating so serious a matter is more tender and intimate than if one hears it at a dinner table or reads it from an invitation.
>
> Of course the man may communicate his good fortune to his intimate few in the same manner. Written responses are made at once and flowers may be sent to the girl by her own or her betrothed's friends. Congratulatory notes are obligatory, but gifts, even of flowers, are not. Sometimes it is pre-determined by the pair, who it is that shall be thus informed of their new relation, and the same persons may be invited to the dinner. In the latter event, the engagement is not mentioned to any who are not guests until after the dinner, when the betrothal is considered public, and congratulations from acquaintances are permissible.
>
> At such dinners of ceremony, the father takes out his engaged daughter, and places her at his right hand, and the mother is escorted by the man soon to be a member of her family. This is the only occasion upon which a father confers this distinguishing honor upon an unwedded young daughter. If the engagement was not mentioned upon the notes of invitation, of course this formality of table-placing prepares guests for what is to come, but

delicacy and good breeding forbid any allusion to such expectations.

If wine is served, the father, rising, lifts his glass and drinks to the health of his son, mentioning the name of his daughter's betrothed's. Every one lifts a wine glass and bows to the betrothed man. Sometimes, after briefly thanking the host and guests, the latter lifts wine glass and bows to his hosts, to their daughter, and to the table generally, and drinks to their happiness. All lift their glasses, and bow to him in return. General congratulation follows before the men are left to their cigars. Of course, every one talks of the pleasant event and predicts happiness and good fortune.

If there is no wine, the host rises and begs to present his future son to his guests. Everybody rises, and a general hand-grasping follows. After this pleasant ceremonial men and women separate for a little time, as when healths are drunk in wine.

To most girls this is a trying social occasion, during which kind and discreet mothers are sure to make the ordeal as easy for their daughters as they are able by controlling their own emotion and maintaining a tranquility that is dignified, though sometimes difficult.

§a §a §a

WHEN mothers or fathers announce by notes engagements in their families, congratulatory responses are written to the writer only, but messages of good will and kindest wishes are sent in the same to the engaged.

Sometimes betrothals are not announced, and invitations to marriages are the first official information there is of a wedding.

This abrupt proceeding is not in the best form. It is treating a marriage as if it were something not quite honorable, or not in good form. If circumstances forbid a ceremonious announcement, a girl may inform her dearest friends by note, or by visiting them, or a mother may do

the same for her; but to make a secret of so serious an affair is not quite dignified.

— Weddings Formal and Informal

Yet, though it wasn't to be secret, neither should it have been the subject of *too* much discussion:

A LOVE affair being the most sacred of all personal matters, it should be spared discussion or criticism; chattering about engagements to the engaged is decidedly coarse. Good form forbids it. But persons of refined sentiment and good breeding do not need to be thus instructed.

An announced engagement justifies no questions from any one outside the immediate family. Kind wishes alone are appropriate speech regarding it between friends and acquaintances of an affianced man or woman.

— Weddings Formal and Informal

THE ENGAGEMENT RING

To mark the momentous event, a ring was often given and received, as it is today, and has been through the ages. The tradition has ancient roots; the Book of Genesis mentions the giving of a ring (by Pharaoh to Joseph) to solemnize and secure an agreement. Greek men gave their beloveds rings on getting engaged, with inscriptions such as this one from the fourth century B.C.: "To her who excels not only in virtue and prudence, but also in wisdom" (Ishee, 24–25).

Various acceptable ring choices are described in an 1891 guide to engagements and weddings:

Engagement Rings.

CUSTOM, rather than obligation, suggests that a ring be offered the woman as a token or emblem of the marriage in the future.

This ceremonial between the two cannot or ought not to occur until both are prepared to acknowledge their intentions.

As a rule, a young woman does not wear a ring on the third finger of her left hand, except it be significant of a betrothal: therefore a postponement of its assumption is proper until the publicity of such a compact is agreeable to both.

There is no etiquette for rings. Only a foolish girl— perhaps only a silly one, is willing to accept an engagement ring that is more costly than is warranted by the financial circumstances of the man she is to marry. It is, of course, natural that a lover should desire to make this gift an expression of the largeness of his devotion, and the delicate-minded girl will appreciate her betrothed's desire to be generous, but she cannot accept an expensive ring, unless the man's fortune justifies him in its purchase. A costly gift from a poor man is sure to provoke comments that are uncomplimentary to giver and receiver.

Not long since a solitaire diamond was almost universally selected for betrothals, its size varying according to discretion or taste. This custom has had many innovations within a few years; rings with significant stones set into them being preferred by many girls that have perfect taste. Moon stones are for luck; sapphires for immortal love; rubies for warm affection, etc., etc. Each stone has its votaries.

Now and then diamonds are set with other stones. Sometimes a circlet of small diamonds is preferred, these little stones reaching around the finger. Diamond circlets are less costly than solitaires of good quality. This circlet need not be of those very small diamonds that are set into guard rings, although these little circlets are not infrequently preferred, because these will serve as protectors, later on, over that more precious circlet of gold which is to be worn always. Many women request that the marriage ring be left on the hand at burial, hence the need of a guard for it. Of course a girl is asked by her lover to

express her preference in stones, if she has one. Sometimes she is urged to choose an engagement ring for herself, but delicacy usually deters her from making this decision. She values most a gift that is wholly one of impulse, and good form approves her delicacy for reasons not necessary to mention.

In some countries a plain gold ring, inscribed with the two names and the date of betrothal, is worn upon the girl's finger, to be removed only on the wedding day, when it is taken off by herself and replaced by the clergyman, after which another one, set with a stone or stones, is added by the husband as a guard.

If one considers only the sentiment of an engagement ring, this custom appears preferable to our own. It spares the maiden the unpleasantness of feeling herself undervalued or over-ornamented by her affianced. Perhaps, since we are shifting our ideals of fitness in the matter of engagement rings, this foreign custom may meet our approval. As was mentioned, this engagement ring is seldom worn, unless the engagement which it typifies is no longer to be a secret; but there are exceptions. If a girl wears a significant ring, and makes no mention of its meaning to her friends, it is very bad form to comment upon it. Confidences should be demanded of no one. Certainly it is in the worst possible taste to suggest confessions of private personal matters.

— *Weddings Formal and Informal*

The popularity of diamonds may stem from the belief that their "sparkle comes from the fires of love" and because their durability symbolized long-lasting love. Italians in the Middle Ages were the first to use diamonds in engagement rings (Ishee, 25–26).

CHAPTER 2

Wedding Plans

&

Once the engagement had been announced according to form, the affianced of polite society, and their families, faced the potentially immense task of planning every detail of their desired wedding ritual. The *Bride's Book of Etiquette* of 1930 advised:

General Plans and Obligations

IN planning a wedding, three factors must be considered—the means and social position of the bride, the groom, and their families; the wishes of the bride and the groom; the dignity which the occasion demands.

Social custom requires that the wedding conform to the position of the persons directly interested. It is the worst possible taste to turn the occasion into an elaborate social function, far beyond the means of the bride's parents. Such weddings invite ridicule. The most beautiful weddings and those which linger longest in the memory of guests are the simplest affairs, so carefully managed that there is no confusion, no evidence of anxiety on the part of the bride or her family.

The wishes of the bride and groom should be consulted next, and their choice between a small, simple wedding and a large function should be accepted. Very often this,

the greatest day in the lives of a young couple, is clouded by the domination or social ambition of a well-meaning but thoughtless and selfish family.

Dignity in appointments, gowning, and conduct of a wedding will endow the occasion with beauty and elegance. Bridal attendants in frocks of violent colorings and extreme styles, heavily rouged faces, and jazz music have no place at a wedding, which is not a pageant or fashion show, but a sacrament.

SETTING THE DATE

The first order of business was to set the date for this "greatest day." By rights, the setting of the date was the mother's domain, on the reasoning that she would have the most to do to prepare for what could be a very grand event. However, in practice:

OF course, the girl confesses a willingness to be married at a certain date before the man asks the mother if she will permit the ceremonial to be at the time mentioned. This is a bit of *finesse*—as a rule—but it is a creditable one. No mother would like to hasten her daughter's departure from her home, but even she who is nearest but no longer dearest, would not venture to suggest a marriage day for her child until she knows her preference.

For this very good reason, it is etiquette for the man to seek the mother's approval of a date that he mentions—of course always with the authority of his *fiancée*. The father is sought when a man desires consent to wed a daughter of the house, but the mother's willingness must be secured for determining the marriage day. The latter may require a longer time to prepare for it, and beg for a delay, and her reasons for such postponement may be more weighty than those of the man who desires to hasten the wedding. Of course mutual concessions establish mutual likings, and no man can afford to be selfishly obstinate with the

family of his future wife, nor will the womanly dignity of an engaged girl allow her to be influenced by unreasonableness against her mother's wishes. Except for serious objections to a delay that is too procrastinating, no manly man will set his own preferences against those of a mother, who has a natural right to have her judgment and convenience duly considered.

In song and romance, the bride is asked to "name the day" and her naming appears, according to this whimsical, or, at least impractical authority, to settle this matter beyond a possible change. Ordinarily the American girl is wise in her generation, and places the date at a fitting remoteness; and importunity for abbreviating the weeks or months intervening before wedlock is of as little avail as if the lover were appealing to a practical mother. This at first appears to be a spirit that is wanting in sentiment, but time proves to the most enthusiastic of lovers that practicality brings content when applied to every day married life, and that it is "sweet reasonableness" only that bestows a charm upon domesticity, when its monotonous duties are once assumed.

— *Weddings Formal and Informal*

The time of day for the ceremony, though variable, was not a matter of free choice. Both social dictum and the realities of the workplace/business world (always a central part of the marriage bond, after all) had their impact:

THE hour of the wedding depends entirely upon the means, the tastes, and the social connections of the parties directly concerned. The most fashionable hour in exclusive circles is 4 P.M. Next in favor comes the noon wedding, and the evening wedding last. Both the high noon and the four-o'clock wedding mean that a man will lose the major part of the business day, so in more democratic circles evening weddings are preferred.

In Catholic circles, the wedding ceremony is often performed as early as nine o'clock in the morning, when a nuptial mass is sung. Girls in moderate circumstances will wisely select the morning wedding followed by a simple breakfast.

—The Bride's Book of Etiquette

OBTAINING THE LICENSE

All the tasks relating to the wedding were assigned, fairly strictly, to either one sex or the other, and it fell to the men to see to getting the legal permit for the marriage.

THE groom secures and pays for the marriage license, and if the state law requires that the bride accompany the groom when the application is made, he consults her convenience as to the hour. Newcomers in a town and romantically inclined couples who wish to be married secretly in a State other than that in which they reside, should investigate carefully the laws governing marriage licenses. Gretna Greens are fast disappearing.

—The Bride's Book of Etiquette

EXPENSES

The first, the last, the cardinal rule of wedding arrangements was that

NO matter what the circumstances, what the difference in the financial status between the bride and groom, what the generosity of attitude of the groom and his family, the wedding must be paid for by the family of the bride or the bride herself.

The groom may be most willing to bear the expenses of the wedding; the groom's parents may be most anxious to have the wedding in their home, perhaps more beautiful

and ample than the bride's; the groom's mother may most affectionately urge the bride to allow her to have the wedding reception in the groom's home. But, obviously, none of these plans is permissible according to the dictates of good form and good taste. The girl with good breeding will wish to adapt her plans to conform to good taste. She will scorn sailing under false colors, and will set to work to plan making what resources she has "fair up to her means."

— Weddings: Modes, Manners and Customs

Should the bride have no parents or other immediate relatives, she was still responsible—solely—for the costs and planning of the wedding day festivities. Given this iron-clad rule, it may have been reassuring to know that:

THIS does not mean, however, that the Cinderella bride will be denied a wedding feast. If she lives in the country or suburbs, the ceremony may be performed in a small church, with simple decorations from woods and fields, or garden flowers contributed by friends. Such a ceremony may be followed by a very simple wedding breakfast at the bride's home, to which are invited only the bridal attendants, the immediate families, and the most intimate friends of the bride and groom. Sandwiches, salad, coffee, and a bride's cake, the last home-made and professionally iced, form an ample menu.

The city girl's problem is more difficult, as a small apartment will rarely accommodate even the families of bride and groom for ceremony and breakfast. A young musician, recently married in New York, set aside exactly one week's earnings for her wedding. The ceremony was performed in the small, picturesque chapel of a famous church, after which a simple breakfast was served to the immediate families of the bride and the groom at a quaint French restaurant.

A girl of moderate means, even a self-supporting girl, who marries into a family of wealth, social standing, and good breeding will find that by doing things simply, in the *right* way, she will find favor in the eyes of her new relatives. Only the newly-rich place a false value on Cinderella's wedding and trousseau and believe that she should keep up appearances at any cost.

— *The Bride's Book of Etiquette*

Just what did the bride's, or bride's family's, obligations entail? The social arbiters' lists were lengthy. Even in the 1930s, according to Emily Post, "a big fashionable wedding [could] total far up in the thousands and even the simplest entail[ed] considerable outlay." Adjusting for means and desires—and Prohibition—a list such as Post's was typical:

The Parents of the Bride Provide:

1. Engraved invitations and cards.

2. The service of a professional secretary who compiles a single list from the various ones sent her, addresses the envelopes, both inner and outer; encloses the proper number of cards, seals, stamps and mails all the invitations. (This item can be omitted and the work done by the family.)

3. The biggest item of expense—the trousseau of the bride, which may consist not alone of wearing apparel of endless variety and lavish detail, but household linen of finest quality (priceless in these days) and in quantity sufficient for a lifetime; or it may consist of the wedding dress, and even that a traveling one, and one or two others, with barest essentials and few accessories.

4. Awnings for church and house. This may be omitted at the house in good weather, at the church, and also in the country.

5. Decorations of church and house. Cost can be eliminated by amateurs using garden or field flowers.

6. Choir, soloists and organist at church. (Choir and soloists unnecessary.)

7. Orchestra at house. (This may mean fifty pieces with two leaders or it may mean a piano, violin and drum, or a violin, harp and guitar.)

8. Carriages or motors for the bridal party from house to church and back.

9. The collation, which may be the most elaborate sit-down luncheon or the simplest afternoon tea.

10. Boxes of wedding cake [typically given to all the guests].

11. Champagne—used to be one of the biggest items, as a fashionable wedding without plenty of it was unheard of. Perhaps though, pocketbooks may have less relief on account of its omission than would at first seem probable, since what is saved on the wine bill is made up for on the additional food necessary to make the best wineless menu seem other than meagre.

12. The bride's presents to her bridesmaids. (May be jewels of value or trinkets of trifling cost.)

13. A wedding present to the bride from each member of her family—not counting her trousseau which is merely part of the wedding.

14. The bride gives a "wedding present" or a "wedding" ring or both to the groom, if she especially wants to. (Not necessary nor even customary.)

—*Etiquette*

There could be numerous other costs also; for example, if a bride chose to employ "carriage callers" at the church.

And it should not be forgotten that the groom and his family had obligations on their side as well. In some circles, the groom's side was considered responsible for the clergyman's fee, which could range from five or ten dollars to over a hundred (in the 1880s; or fifty to several hundred in the 1920s), and for conveying the best man to the church or house for the ceremony. The vehicle used then would usually also be the one to take the bride, now the wife and no longer traveling under her parents' auspices, from the church to the reception and to take the newlyweds from the reception.

In one famous instance, the groom took on all the wedding arrangements while his bride, Frances Folsom, was in Europe on her pre-wedding trip with her mother. The man was Grover Cleveland and the wedding took place in the middle of his first term as president, no less. Folsom's father was dead, and her grandfather, at whose home the wedding was to have taken place, died while Folsom was traveling. Though held at the White House, the wedding was small and considered "quiet." Even so, there was a profusion of details, as the following description shows. Even if President Cleveland had some assistance from a staff member or two, that would not have set him apart from the wealthier brides and mothers-of-the-bride of his day, and it was still unusual for a man to involve himself with the "woman's" side of things.

EVERYTHING to do with the new arrangements received his personal attention, from the writing of the invitations to the music and the flowers. The very few Cabinet members, relatives and friends who were invited received simple hand-written notes dated only five days before the wedding:

My dear Mr. ——
I am to be married on Wednesday evening at seven o'clock at the White House to Miss Folsom. It will be a very quiet affair and I will be extremely gratified at your attendance on the occasion.
Yours sincerely,
Grover Cleveland.

By Presidential edict, floral bells and horseshoes were forbidden, but some thwarted artist managed to add the date, 2 June 1886, in yellow pansies (the figures nearly a foot high) to the permitted monograms. When it came to music, the President was able to turn to John Philip Sousa, director of the Marine Band, for assistance. Looking back on his life later, (*Marching Along*, 1928), Sousa recalled suggesting a piece from one of his own operas, *Désirée*, as part of the incidental music for the evening—a quartette called *The Student of Love*. Studying the proposed programme, the 49-year-old, portly, bachelor bridegroom said with executive decision: 'I think I'd play that number just as "A quartette," leaving out "The Student of Love".' . . .

The bride was smuggled back into the country at the end of her Atlantic voyage, and a few days later, at 5:30 A.M., arrived in Washington on the morning of her wedding day—with the *trousseau* she had chosen in Paris. . . . There were no bridesmaids, and the President himself, wearing a black dress suit, led the bride into the Blue Room of the White House; there, beneath the central gas-lit chandelier they were married by the Reverent Byron Sunderland of the First Presbyterian Church, and, on this unlikely occasion, the word 'obey' was purposely omitted from the bride's vows. Sousa conducted Mendelssohn's *Wedding March* for their entrance and Wagner's *Bridal Chorus* for their exit. Church bells pealed out all over Washington, whistles blew, and the cannons in the Navy yard were fired in salute. Outside, the crowds, who had been allowed to wander over the White House lawns to the portico of the main entrance, cheered.

Supper was served in the small family dining-room, which like the other reception rooms had been turned into a bower of flowers (one of the fireplaces in the Oval Room was full of flowing begonias, with Centaureas scattered on the hearth beneath like ashes); the centre-piece of the supper table was a three-masted floral schooner—the 'Hymen'—with a flag for each mast: the stars and stripes on

the main mast and C-F in gold on the others. Each guest had gifts of sweetmeats in satin bags and a satin-covered box of wedding cake, with a hand-painted spray of flowers on the lid, and a card signed personally by both bride and groom (a box and card—rare trophies from this select gathering—can still be seen at the Smithsonian Institution.)

—And the Bride Wore . . .

For most grooms and their families, the list of wedding items to arrange and pay for would typically consist of only the following:

The Groom's Expenses Are:

1. The engagement ring—as handsome as he can possibly afford.
2. A wedding present—jewels if he is able, always something for her personal adornment [which she would usually wear as part of her going-away ensemble].
3. His bachelor dinner.
4. The marriage license.
5. A personal gift to his best man and each of his ushers.
6. To each of the above he gives their wedding ties, gloves and boutonniéres.
7. The bouquet carried by the bride. In many cities it is said to be the custom for the bride to send boutonniéres to the ushers and for the groom to order the bouquets of the bridesmaids. In New York's smart world, the bridesmaids' bouquets are looked upon as part of the decorative arrangement, all of which is in the province of the bride's parents.
8. The wedding ring.
9. The clergyman's fee.

—Etiquette

But in the end, Post reminds us, in polite society:

> 10. From the moment the bride and groom start off on their wedding trip, all the expenditure becomes his.

CHAPTER 3

Wedding Invitations
and
Announcements

୫ଥ

COMPILING THE GUEST LIST

FOUR persons contribute names to the invitation list
for a large wedding—the bride and her mother, the groom
and his mother. In case either the bride or the groom has
no mother, the family list is compiled by a near relative
who knows the names of family connections and friends.
For a small wedding, when the bride writes informal
notes of invitation, she and the groom decide who shall be
invited, bearing in mind, of course, the courtesy due families on both sides.

Let us consider the long list first. The mother of the
bride and the mother of the groom turn in their visiting
lists. The bride lists her friends who may or may not be
included among the calling acquaintances of the two
mothers. The groom furnishes a list of his business or professional friends, his classmates at college, and his friends
in other cities whom he would like to have at his wedding.
These lists are compared to avoid duplication of names. If
the list is very long and the bride's family have means, the
list is then turned over to a social secretary, who verifies
the addresses, writes the name of the guest in the blank
space on the invitation, addresses the double envelopes,

seals and posts the invitations on the appointed day, usually three weeks before the date set for the wedding. The invitations must all go out at the same time. Stationers will supply names of social secretaries who do this type of work by the hour.

When the list is smaller and the family's social life less pretentious, various members of a large family fill in and address the invitations. Even the groom sometimes participates. When the wedding is so small that invitations are not engraved, the bride writes each invitation personally.

For a church wedding followed by a reception each name must be checked for invitations to church or house or both. If the ceremony at the church is to be witnessed by family and intimate friends only, the majority of the invitations will be for the reception at the house. On the other hand, if a large number can be accommodated in the church and only a few at the house, the greater number of invitations will be for the ceremony and a limited number for the reception and the breakfast. Another checking of the list will indicate which invitations are to contain the cards for pews specially numbered or bearing the phrase "Within the ribbons."

Within the Ribbons

Thursday the fifth of December

In the average family, it is wise to start compiling the list at an early date. Last-minute lists are never satisfactory because, in the haste, friends are forgotten, and many a social feud has been started by just this sort of carelessness.

Whatever the social ambition of the bride and the groom and of their families, whatever changes may have overtaken their fortunes, a wedding list never betrays snobbishness or lack of consideration for old friends. Unless there has been an actual quarrel, even relatives and family friends, now rarely seen, are invited to weddings. It is also a gracious custom to send invitations to old servants of either family, and to the seamstresses who have worked on the bride's trousseau.

— *The Bride's Book of Etiquette*

Life being simpler then (and perhaps the Postal Service speedier), three or even two week before the wedding was generally the recommended time for mailing the invitations.

INVITATIONS TO AN INFORMAL WEDDING

INFORMAL invitations to informal weddings may be given by word of mouth, telephone, or note, according to the number of people to be asked, the kind of ceremony contemplated, and the pleasure of the family. Suppose two young people choose to be married almost in private, either in the house or at church. Their immediate families and the best friends of both might not amount to a dozen people. It would be absurd to think of having invitations engraved for so simple an occasion; even for twice the number it would not be necessary.

Those to whom it is of real interest, like the near relations, will have been told the day and hour, and to so small a company of intimate friends as has been suggested notes could be sent, if necessary. These should come from the bride's mother (or possibly an aunt or elder sister —

whoever gives the wedding and breakfast) or should be sent in her name. At any social entertainment the mistress of the house, and not the girl, is considered hostess. Of course, if the bride should be the daughter of a widower and living in his house she would invite people in his name. Only in families whose pretensions to gentility are confined to the younger generation are older people ignored. And this relegating of parents to the background is a sure sign of ill breeding.

Some examples of informal notes follow.

MY DEAR MRS. BROWN:

Mathilda is to be married at home on Monday, the twenty-fourth, at twelve o'clock. We hope very much that you and Mr. Brown will come to the wedding and to the very informal breakfast afterward.

Most sincerely yours,

LUCY MAYLY.

This, let us say, is from Mrs. Mayly to a friend of the groom's family, whom she knows but slightly. She would probably call a friend of her own by her Christian name. If a bride wrote for her mother the wording might be something like this.

MY DEAR MRS. JONES:

I am to be married at St. Mary's Chapel on Monday, the twenty-fourth, at half-past twelve. Mama asks me to say how much she hopes both you and Jane will be there and will come afterward to the small breakfast we are having for our families and a few friends.

Yours very sincerely,

AMY LYNDON.

In place of the mother's name, "my father," or "Papa," or "my aunt," or "my sister," might appear. Both notes, while informal, are written less casually than they would be to near relations or intimate friends, for whom something rather in the nature of a message would be sufficient. Conventional two-sheeted notepaper should be

used. It will be noticed that the month is not mentioned in giving the date and time of the wedding, and this is because the invitations for such a simple ceremony would be sent out perhaps only a week, or even a few days, before. The month could be added if there were any possibility of mistake.

—Vogue's Book of Brides

For Example:

Molly dearest:

    Jim and I are to be married on Wednesday the eleventh, at St. Paul's, Hillsdale-on-Hudson, at half-past twelve. Of course we want you and yours with us on this day. Later Aunt Helen is having us all at her home, which you know is just a block from the church, for cake, cup, and good luck. We are counting on you.

Affectionately,
Jane Tilton

Dear Mr. Grant:

    Jim and I are to be married at 12 noon, Wednesday, the eleventh, in the chapel of St. Paul's Church, East 24th Street. We want a few of our old friends with us on this occasion and Jim counts you as one of these. After the ceremony, we hope you will join us for the informal breakfast which my mother is giving for us at the Crillion.

Faithfully yours,
Jane Tilton

—The Bride's Book of Etiquette

INVITATIONS TO A FORMAL WEDDING

For a formal wedding, the matter of invitations was considerably more complex and weighty.

THE invitations are issued in the name of the bride's parents, parent, or nearest relative; they are handsomely engraved in script, with coats of arms, crest or monogram, or without, as pleases the parties in interest; the envelope should be a distinctive wedding envelope, not a wedding invitation sent in a reception style of envelope. If crest, coats of arms, or monogram are used on the invitations, they should be used also on the envelopes. The quality and tint of the invitations, At Home, Church Cards, and inside Envelopes, should be the same, not, as often seen, each a color of its own, which spoils their entirety and beauty. The invitations, At Home and Church Card, are enclosed in the same wedding envelope, on which is written names only of the parties to whom you are sending them, then enclosed in an outside envelope, on which is written full name and address, which is sent by mail to ensure positive delivery.

It is often debated as to which is correct in the wording of invitations —

Request your presence —

Request your company — or,

Request the honor of your company —

Request your presence is correct.

Webster defines *Presence*, "the existence of a person in a certain place;" *Company*, "to accompany, to be companion to;" *Honor*, "to reverence, exalt, dignify, glorify, etc." We wish to imply, that we should be pleased to have them present to witness the marriage; not to accompany us; or to be our companions on that occasion. We do not expect them to reverence us, neither do we mean to imply that their presence will be necessary to make the occasion illustrious.

It is often questioned, which is correct — to, or and — as in forms —

Miss Georgia to Mr. Auguste Clarendon; or, Miss Georgia and Mr. Auguste Clarendon.

To, is accepted as the proper word. The lady is married to the gentleman, receiving his name and becoming his consort.

— *Wedding Etiquette and Usages of Polite Society*

Fifty years later, in the 1930s, the conventions in polite society governing what constituted a correct formal wedding invitation remained much the same.

FOR the formal wedding an engraved invitation is essential. The formal invitation, which is always written in the third person and in the name of the parents or nearest of kin to the bride, requires two envelopes. The inner envelope has no gum on the flap, is never sealed, and bears the name of the person or persons addressed thus:

Mr. and Mrs. Jonathan Wood

The outer envelope, slightly larger, which is to be sealed, is addressed thus:

Mr. and Mrs. Jonathan Wood,
2400 Euclid Avenue,
Cleveland, Ohio

The wedding invitation is engraved on a double sheet of paper, 5⅛ inches wide by 7⅜ inches deep. The color is white, the engraving black. The present vogue calls for paper of a deep, rich cream-white tone rather than dead white. Unless the bride's family boasts a crest there must be no device, and the crest, if used, must be embossed in white.

The most elaborate form of invitation is required when the ceremony takes place in a church, and a reception or breakfast follows at home or hotel. First there is an invitation to the church with the card of admittance, and for relatives and intimates, a second and smaller card indicating that the holder is to be seated in a certain pew, or at least within the white ribbons. For a country-house wedding, a train card is also inclosed so that guests from town may travel on a specified train, possibly in a special car.

FORM 1

Mr. and Mrs. James Wells Stanhope

request the honor of

presence at the marriage of their daughter

Hortense

to

Mr. Howard Ames Moore

on Thursday the fifth of December

at twelve o'clock

at Saint Luke's Church

and afterwards at

Nine East Twelfth Street

R.s.v.p.

FORM 2

Mr. and Mrs. James Wells Stanhope

request the honor of your presence

at the marriage of their daughter

Hortense

to

Mr. Howard Ames Moore

on Thursday, the fifth of December

at twelve o'clock noon

Saint Luke's Church

and afterwards at

Nine East Twelfth Street

R.s.v.p.

The first form is the more formal.

CARD OF ADMITTANCE TO THE CHURCH

Please present this card at

Saint Luke's Church

on Thursday the fifth of December

CARDS FOR RESERVED PEWS

Please present this card to an usher

Pew No. ....

on Thursday the fifth of December

or

Pew 8

Mrs. James Wells Stanhope

Nine East Twelfth Street

or

Within the Ribbons

Thursday the fifth of December

CARD FOR TRAIN INFORMATION FOR
COUNTRY WEDDING

A special train will leave the Union Station at

11 A.M. arriving at Sunnyside at 11:30 A.M.

Returning train will leave Sunnyside at 2:30 P.M.

arriving at Union Station at 3 P.M.

If a special car is provided, this line must be added to the above form:

Show this card at the gate

If the number of guests invited to the church ceremony is very large and the number invited to the house is limited, they are divided in the following way: those expected at both church and house receive with the invitation to the ceremony at the church a card of admittance and, in case of a country wedding, a train card, and still a third card which fits exactly into the inner envelope, inviting them to the reception and the wedding breakfast. The less privileged receive invitations to the church only.

INVITATION TO CHURCH CEREMONY ONLY

Mr. and Mrs. James Wells Stanhope

request the honor of

presence at the marriage of their daughter

Hortense

to

Mr. Howard Ames Moore

on Thursday the fifth of December

at four o'clock

at Saint Luke's Church

in the City of Cleveland

INVITATION TO BREAKFAST OR RECEPTION ONLY

Mr. and Mrs. James Wells Stanhope

request the pleasure of your company

at the wedding breakfast of their daughter

Hortense

and

Mr. Howard Ames Moore

on Thursday, the fifth of December

at one o'clock

at Nine East Twelfth Street

The favor of an answer
is requested
        or
R.s.v.p.

If it is a house wedding, only one invitation is necessary. Anyone invited to the ceremony is naturally expected to remain to the reception and breakfast.

Mr. and Mrs. James Wells Stanhope

request the honor of your presence

at the marriage of their daughter

Hortense

to

Mr. Howard Ames Moore

on Thursday the fifth of December

at twelve o'clock

at Nine East Twelfth Street

R.s.v.p.

There are occasions when the ceremony in the home is witnessed by members of the family only, as when the mother or some other member of the family is an invalid. In such a case the few relatives who witness the ceremony are invited personally by letter, or word of mouth, while invitations for the breakfast and the reception are engraved and sent out in the two envelopes like the regular invitations for a house wedding. See Form 1.

If a girl's father is dead and her mother is living, the invitations are issued in the mother's name, thus:

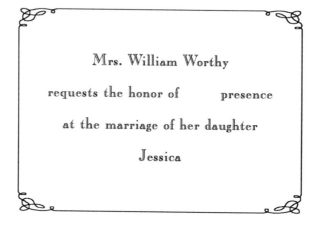

Mrs. William Worthy

requests the honor of   presence

at the marriage of her daughter

Jessica

If the mother is dead, the father issues the invitations.

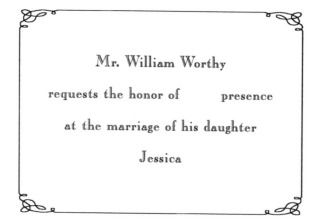

Mr. William Worthy

requests the honor of   presence

at the marriage of his daughter

Jessica

If both parents are dead, the invitation must be issued in the name of a brother or sister, preferably married, thus:

Mr. and Mrs. William Worthy

request the honor of   presence

at the marriage of their sister

Jessica

Invitations may also be issued in the name of an uncle or an aunt of the bride.

If a girl has no relatives and still wishes to have a formal wedding, the invitations may be issued by her resident chaperon and are worded thus:

Miss Priscilla Doolittle

requests the honor of   presence

at the marriage of Miss Jessica Worthy

If she has made her home with friends and become a member of their family, the invitation may be issued in the name of this couple. However, a girl in this position usually has a quiet, informal wedding.

How are invitations worded for a double wedding?

Mr. and Mrs. James Wells Stanhope

request the honor of your presence

at the marriage of their daughters

Hortense

to

Mr. Howard Ames Moore

and

Mildred

to

Mr. Theodore Buckley

on Thursday the fifth of December

at twelve o'clock

at Nine East Twelfth Street

R.s.v.p.

—The Bride's Book of Etiquette

Other formal weddings required different variations on the model:

FORM OF FORMAL INVITATION
(To be engraved in Script or Roman Letters)

Mr. and Mrs. Charles Francis Lane

request the honour of your presence

at the marriage of Mrs. Lane's daughter

Clara Louise

to

Mr. James Stow Givingston

on Tuesday, December the fourth

at St. Paul's Chapel

at twelve o'clock

and afterward at breakfast

at No. 9 East Barrack Street

THIS is a form which invites the recipient to church and house together. It will be noticed that the bride is mentioned as Mrs. Lane's daughter, which shows that her father is not Mr. Lane. It is not always considered absolutely necessary to give her last name in the invitation, even though it makes relationship clearer, for the acquaintances to whom it goes are naturally supposed to know a certain amount about the history of their hostess, but, if preferred, the whole name could be given. It depends upon how far outside one's intimates one goes. The substitution of "*Mr.* Lane's daughter" would show that the present Mrs. Lane was not the mother of the bride. This version of the invitation form need not be given, since it is exactly the same as that for Mrs. Lane's daughter.

Wedding invitations are sometimes formal and yet written by hand when the wedding is both small and formal; an example is given of such an invitation.

Mr. and Mrs. William Philips James

request the honour of

Mr. Edwards'

presence at the marriage of their daughter

Marianne Bertha

to

Mr. Henry Thomas Pearson

on Tuesday, the fourth of December

at half after four o'clock

269 Lincoln Avenue

New York

R.S.V.P.

—Vogue's Book of Brides

Exhaustive as these guidelines may seem, there were still other important considerations in the preparation of invitations.

LET it be said here that whether tissue paper is, or isn't found in the invitations doesn't make one earthly bit of difference! Very particular people, having made sure that the engraving ink is dry, like to have the tissue paper taken out. Others, fearing the ink may still be wet and the invitations blurred, leave the tissue paper in. There is nothing "smart" about leaving it (as some people have imagined)—rather the contrary—but neither is there any disgrace in its being left. And in the hurry-scurry of today it generally is.

How to Address Invitations

Many questions are asked about addressing invitations. They are never to be directed to "Mr. Brown and family." That is one absolute rule. "Mr. and Mrs. John Brown" will have an envelope of their own. Whether both are known to the sender or not the invitation should always go to man and wife. If there are two or three daughters they may be addressed as "The Misses Brown," or as "Miss Anne Brown, Miss Beatrice Brown, Miss Celia Brown." It is not necessary to address an elder daughter separately if all the girls are asked, but the elder might be invited alone. Indeed, at a small wedding, which ever member of the household is most intimate with the bride or groom might be chosen to represent the family. To a large general wedding all would be asked. If there were several young men among the Browns they would be addressed as "The Messrs. Brown."

Types of Lettering

Lettering is another frequently discussed subject, but beyond warning people against choosing the too elaborate this must be left to their own taste. There are, from time to time, slight differences in fashion. One year the mode may turn more decidedly toward English script; another

year toward simple Roman, or shaded modified Roman, or shaded Antique Roman. The smaller type, neatly spaced, so that it has form in the middle of a page with adequate border, seems the most conservatively safe selection. Some lettering is rather confusing. The more easily anything *to* be read *can* be read, the better. Invitations must be engraved, never printed. The same is true of announcements. If such customs cannot be followed according to their traditions it is much more sensible to adopt different ones, suitable to conditions that are not (and should not be) hampered by the ways of society in its more formal phases.

— Vogue's Book of Brides

Acceptances and Regrets

Styles of invitations to weddings may not have changed much from the Gay Nineties to the Roaring Twenties and beyond, but customs concerning replies decidedly did.

In the nineteenth century, one was advised that:

> It is questionable if any breach of etiquette is so general as that of permitting invitations to weddings to go without acknowledgment. If the courtesy of sending you an invitation has been extended, it is a mark of ignorance or ill-breeding to allow it to remain unnoticed. A form of acknowledgment now in favor is, with each wedding invitation an envelope is sent, printed on the flap: "Please present at the church with your card enclosed." If parties receiving same do not attend the church, then the cards should be sent to residence. If the envelope is not enclosed with the invitation, your card should be enclosed in an envelope and sent by mail. A favor worthy of reception, is worthy of an acknowledgement.

— Wedding Etiquette and Usages of Polite Society

By 1930, "an invitation to the church ceremony requires no acknowledgment," one arbiter of taste categorically stated. However, another specified:

> TO the invitation to a large church wedding, where practically every acquaintance is asked, it is not necessary to send an answer unless the guest has reason to think a special place in a certain pew is reserved. But to a small church wedding, where every seat is arranged for, an answer should be sent as soon as possible. All these customs are the result of consideration. When seats are being reserved for certain people it is awkward not to know whether or not they are coming. A card with the number of the pew is generally posted after an acceptance has been received.
>
> *— Vogue's Book of Brides*

And all agreed that

> TO *reception* invitations an answer is *always* expected. How else can a hostess know for how many guests she must provide space and refreshments?
>
> *— Vogue's Book of Brides*

Whether the invitations were handwritten or engraved, replies were always handwritten in a formal style. Both acceptances and regrets were expected.

> ANSWERS to wedding invitations must be carefully written and spaced to follow the form of engraved ones. It is not necessary to repeat every word, although the form is copied. A double-sheeted piece of formal notepaper is always used; never a card.

In formal answers it is not necessary to give reasons for inability to be present as it is when refusing an informal invitation. If the guest is on intimate terms with the family an explanation would be more courteous but could be made by word of mouth or friendly message. The formal answer would go just the same to be listed with the other acceptances and refusals.

It should be unnecessary to say that formal invitations and replies like those given, written in the third person, are never either signed or dated, yet it must be said, for the question has been asked. In the examples of answers it will be seen that the names of bride and bridegroom are not repeated, otherwise the wording is practically the same as that of the invitation. The reason for repeating the date and time is to show that they have been noted.

Mr. Edwards

has much pleasure

in accepting

the kind invitation of ____

Mr. and Mrs. William Philips James

on Thursday, December the sixth

at half after four o'clock

269 Lincoln Avenue

Mr. and Mrs. Van Zant Gray

accept with pleasure

Mr. and Mrs. Charles Francis Lane's

Kind invitation

to the wedding of Mrs. Lane's daughter

on Tuesday, December the fourth

at twelve o'clock

and afterward at the breakfast

at 9 East Barrack Street.

Mr. and Mrs. John Brown

regret extremely

that they are unable to be present

at the wedding and reception of

Mr. and Mrs. Horsingham Field's

daughter

on Monday, September the tenth

at Brookville

The Misses Brawn

very much regret

that they cannot accept

Mr. and Mrs. Horsingham Field's

kind invitation to

the wedding of their daughter

on Monday, September the tenth

at Brookville

—*Vogue's Book of Brides*

For an informal wedding with informal invitations, replies in kind were appropriate.

MY DEAR MRS. MAYLY:

My husband and I accept with pleasure your very kind invitation to be present at your daughter's wedding, on Monday, the twenty-fourth, and at breakfast afterward.

Very sincerely yours,

JANET BROWN.

MY DEAR AMY:

Jane and I regret so much that we shall be away on the twenty-fourth. We are paying a long-promised visit to my sister. We are sincerely disappointed to miss the wedding. My kind regards to your mother and a thousand good wishes to you.

Affectionately yours,

EMILY JONES.

—Vogue's Book of Brides

WHEN the wedding is to be small and intimate, and invitations are written by the bride, these must be acknowledged in the same cordial, intimate spirit.

Dearest Mary:

Jim and I are so happy at being asked to your wedding at St. Luke's Church. We will be there, and at your aunt's breakfast later, to wish you all the joy in the world.

Affectionately,

Jane

—The Bride's Book of Etiquette

ANNOUNCEMENTS

For both formal and informal weddings, whether large or small, the practice of sending individual announcements provided a conventional, accepted way to give people not on the guest list, but who may have had an interest, with early and personal notice of the new union.

But one's circles needed to have been large enough, and sufficiently socially significant, to be worthy of the effort.

IF the families of the bride and groom happen to have large lists of acquaintances to whom they feel it necessary to send announcements they will have such announcements engraved, well ahead of the wedding, and send them out on the day. It is not customary to post them before. No matter how small is the bridal company the announcements may be, and often are, sent to a large circle. Society has a habit of letting all its associates know whom its children have married, even if it hasn't been able to ask them to witness the event. But the custom is not one to be followed by everybody. It is expensive and troublesome, and not in the least appropriate to people who are living quiet lives in quiet, unsophisticated surroundings, and whose marryings and givings in marriage are distinctly their own business and that of their nearest and dearest only.

FORM OF FORMAL ANNOUNCEMENT
(To be engraved in Script or Roman Letters)

> *Doctor Robert Foster Leigh*
> *has the honour of announcing*
> *the marriage of his sister*
> *Millicent Anne*
>
> *to*
>
> *Mr. Paul Stuyvesant Barnes*
> *on Tuesday, the second of October*
> *One thousand, nine hundred and twenty-eight*
> *in the City of New York*

—*Vogue's Book of Brides*

Similarly:

WEDDING ANNOUNCEMENTS

Mr. & Mrs. Albert A. Grossmann
announce the marriage of their daughter
Dorothea Marguerite,
to
Dr. Frank Fremont Smith,
Thursday, June fifth,
eighteen hundred and ninety.
New York

Mr. & Mrs. James L. Ensign
announce the marriage of their niece,
Miss Sophia Horton,
to
Dr. Leander Young Ketcham,
Tuesday, June the seventeenth, 1890.
New Haven, Conn.

— Wedding Etiquette and Usages of Polite Society

Announcements also provided an opportunity to inform the recipients of the couple's future address, for example:

Mr. and Mrs. Bellamy Hart

Will be at home
after the first of October   *31 Sunshine Terrace*

OR they may inclose their joint visiting card, thus:

Mr. and Mrs. Bellamy Hart

At home
after October first   *31 Sunshine Terrace*

---

with "at home after October first" written in the lower left-hand corner. All wedding announcements are posted on the day of the wedding.

— *The Bride's Book of Etiquette*

And the announcement of the wedding and the new address could be combined on the same card:

WEDDING ANNOUNCEMENT

> *Mr. J. E. Mitchell*
> *Miss Maude E. Halsell,*
> *Married*
> *Wednesday, June the eighteenth,*
> *eighteen hundred and ninety.*
> *Decatur, Texas*

WEDDING ANNOUNCEMENT AND AT HOME

> *Mr. Edward D. Bradford,*
> *Miss Mary L. Gardner,*
> *Married,*
> *Tuesday, July the twenty second, 1890.*
> *New York City*
>
> *At Home*
> *after September first,*
> *1000 K. Street,*
> *Washington, D.C.*

— Wedding Etiquette and Usages of Polite Society

A newlywed man might send out a simple announcement himself:

Mr. James Wood Quintard,

Miss Antoinette Ropes,

Married

—Wedding Etiquette and Usages of Polite Society

While announcements required no answers, the "very polite" might leave or send their visiting cards in acknowledgment. For the wider world, a report of the proceedings, after the fact, could be published in a newspaper, as is often done today.

Though small, private weddings were quite acceptable, keeping a wedding entirely under wraps was not. Elopement and other forms of sudden or secretive marriage did go on, though, prompting these guidelines from *Weddings Formal and Informal*:

> IT is a very rare occurrence when there are reasons sufficiently weighty for keeping a marriage secret.
>
> This does not mean that there should be no marriages where there are but a few witnesses, or no marriages unexpectedly made. Circumstances not infrequently justify and consecrate hasty nuptials, but even in case of such abrupt marriages, they should be lifted to the highest dignity and solemnity by a refined taste, which is only another name for good form.
>
> A secret marriage is always bad form; that is, a marriage that is not at once announced to such as by family or other ties have a right to know of it, whenever circumstances persuade a betrothed pair that it is wisest and

kindest to marry at once. Men have insisted upon an immediate marriage with an invalid, and women have done the same, in order that the strong may be of use to the weak. An unanticipated necessity for the man to remove to a distant country, a death in the family, or other serious reasons, may urge hasty marriages between persons already betrothed, and an announcement of the same is made immediately. Self-respect, dignity, refined taste, good form and etiquette, each and all demand it. This announcement may be made only to those who are nearly concerned, leaving them to mention it to others, but the usual advertisement of such marriages should appear very soon thereafter. A reason given by an authority in such matters for a brief delay, of perhaps a fortnight, but not longer than that, before publishing private marriages, is that such information should first reach the immediate circle of the married couple, and thus spare friends from that unpleasant shock of surprise, and sometimes also, those painful speculations or gossip that naturally follow so unexpected an event, if first made known through the newspapers.

If possible, it is better for the parents or guardians of a bride to send out at the earliest moment after a hasty marriage engraved notes, informing acquaintances of the ceremony. This is done in their own names and implies a family approval.

When the Wedding Was Called Off

Only a serious event justifies recalling wedding invitations, such as the death of a parent or of a very close relative of the bride or groom, or the sudden financial failure of the bride's father. In either case the ceremony is performed privately, with only the necessary witnesses present. Under no circumstances can a small family wedding be substituted for a large one. In very rare instances an engagement is broken after the wedding invitations have

been issued. In such a case any wedding presents must be returned when the invitations are recalled.

The invitations may be recalled by means of a printed card in simple script, which can be delivered by a printer on the same day as ordered. The card should be of the size known as correspondence cards and only one envelope is required. The announcement reads something like this:

> *Owing to the sudden death of Mr. William Worthy, Jr., Mr. and Mrs. William Worthy recall the invitations issued for the wedding of their daughter Jessica.*

One of these cards must go to each person who has received an invitation and, in the interest of safety, a note should be sent to each of the daily papers.

— *The Bride's Book of Etiquette*

It was not necessary to give the reason for the cancellation; that was left to the discretion of the parties concerned. A simple statement such as:

> *Mr. and Mrs. Stephen Orris*
> *regret that they must recall*
> *the invitation to*
> *their daughter's wedding*
> *on Saturday, November the fifteenth.*

— *Vogue's Book of Brides*

was sufficient. In fact, noted *Vogue,* "The briefer such notices the better. They naturally need no answer."

CHAPTER 4

The Ring

Like engagement rings, wedding rings have a long history. Stretching back to ancient Egypt, this history has been interwoven through the centuries with a tapestry of myths and legends, so that today a simple gold band bears a rich, deeply felt array of meanings and hopes for those who wear it. The same was true for nineteenth-century Americans:

THE BRIDAL RING.

AMONG all the rings which ladies wear, no one has attached to it the dignity and honor of the wedding ring. When it first came into use is perhaps not so very clear; but Mr. Waterton says; "The fyancel or wedding-ring is, doubtless, of Roman origin, and was usually given at the betrothal as a pledge of the engagement!" This is very likely correct, for Juvenal, at the commencement of the Christian era, says that a man placed a ring upon the finger of the lady whom he betrothed.

It has been conjectured as an explanation of the bridal ring that as the delivery of a signet-ring to any person was a sign of confidence, so the delivery of a ring by the intended husband to the wife indicated that she was admitted to his confidence. Other explanations are, that

the ring is a symbol of eternity and constancy, and that it was placed on the left hand of the woman to denote her subjection, and on the ring finger because it pressed a vein which communicated directly with the heart.

The plain hoop gold, the precious fetter which now links the worldly fortunes of the wedded pair, has left no record of its introduction.

Poets have made the wedding ring their frequent theme; and so universal is the custom of wearing it among the Jews and Christians that no married woman likes to be without it, or is not found to view it as the best of her personal ornaments.

What the gentlemen think of it may be gathered from the well-known and good old song, from which we are tempted to quote a verse:

> I dreamt last night of our earlier days,
>   Ere I sighed for sword and feather,
> When we danced on the hill in the moon's
>   pale rays
>   Hand in hand together;
> I thought you gave me again that kiss,
>   More sweet than the perfume of spring,
> When I pressed on your finger love's pure
>   golden pledge —
>   The bridal ring! the bridal ring!

From the imperial palace to the lowliest cot this ring is the symbol of wedded life and constancy. Queens and princesses wear it, and in its simplest form count it not beneath their dignity. The small amount of decoration which it may, in some cases, receive, is not regarded as a necessity. What is necessary is the bridal ring, which, by the law of the English Church, must be produced at the marriage ceremony, and must be placed by the bridegroom upon the fourth finger of the left hand of the bride.

—Home Journal.

— Wedding Etiquette and Usages of Polite Society

A ring for the bride was not always required, however:

> THE only essential variation allowable is in the use or
> disuse of a ring in the ceremonies performed by clergy-
> men who are neither Episcopalians nor Roman Catholics.
> In the two church organizations mentioned, a ring is
> obligatory. In others it is not, but may be used if the bride
> requests it, and usually she does. Sometimes rings are
> placed upon the hands of both bride and groom, but this
> is not common.
>
> *— Weddings Formal and Informal*

By the 1920s our modern custom of having both partners in the
marriage give, receive, and wear a ring, "not common" in 1891, was
beginning to spread, and the following advice was available to those
considering the practice:

> WHEN the groom has a wedding ring, who buys it?
> The bride, unless she can give the groom a ring which has
> been an heirloom among the men of her family for gener-
> ations. This exchange of wedding rings is largely a matter
> of nationality, or local custom, or of sentiment between
> the bride and groom.
>
> *— The Bride's Book of Etiquette*

Profoundly symbolic as they were (and are), a ring was something
to be worn, and should reflect the good taste of the bride and groom:

> IT is quite good form for the bride to go with the
> groom when he buys the wedding ring and to express her
> preference as to width, weight, and size. At present, plat-
> inum or white gold is in vogue. The diamond circlet is
> also used when the means and social position of bride and
> groom make it practical. The best form of engraving is the
> date and the initials of the bride and the groom.
>
> *— The Bride's Book of Etiquette*

A Brief History of Wedding Rings

RINGS as symbols of authority have come down to us through the ages. The wedding ring is believed to have evolved from the engagement ring. Wedding rings were given in the days of marriage by purchase both as partial payment and as a symbol of the prospective groom's good intentions.

Some believe that the wedding ring is simply the miniature of the fetters placed on the girl's hands and feet during the days when brides were captured rather than wooed. According to this belief, the use of the circular shape as symbolic of eternity developed much later.

❧ ❧ ❧

THE wedding ring is placed on the third finger of the left hand because it was believed that this finger is connected directly to the heart by the "vena amoris," or vein of love. But most fingers of both hands, including the thumb, have been used for wedding rings in the past. During the Elizabethan period in England, the wedding ring was worn on the thumb, as is shown in oil paintings of ladies of that time. In traditional Jewish weddings, the ring is placed on the first finger of the left hand.

❧ ❧ ❧

Some women refuse to remove their wedding rings after they have been placed on their fingers—left there as a seal of the marriage bond.

—Wedding Toasts and Traditions

CHAPTER 5

Attire for the
Bride and Groom

ℰᔿ

THE BRIDE'S ENSEMBLE

THE DRESS

"Everyone knows what a wedding dress is like," pronounced Emily
Post in the first edition of *Etiquette*, and succinctly summarized its universal similarities and infinite variety: "It may be of any white material, satin, brocade, velvet, chiffon or entirely of lace. It may be
embroidered in pearls, crystals or silver; or it may be as plain as a slip-
cover—anything in fact that the bride fancies, and made in whatever
fashion or period she may choose."

Brides in 1922 had a great deal of fashion options to choose from,
even if they looked back only a few decades or to their own day.
According to fashion historian Alice Lea Mast Tasman, "In the latter
nineteenth and early twentieth centuries, the fashion was to pile on
ornamentation, and designers seemed to vie with one another in
decking their wedding gowns with as much fringe, braid, pleated
ruffling, shirring, lace and other embellishments as the yardage could
encompass." For example: "ivory-figured silk with a lace veil,"
"looped, fringed, pleat-trimmed gray taffeta," and a dress of "gold-
figured silk . . . trimmed with white fringed satin and gold-covered
balls . . . white shirred satin with gold folds at the front of the skirt. . . .
[and a] train has a wide white satin pleat trimmed with white fringed

satin ruffling and bows and lace edging." However, Tasman notes, "From the 1870s to the end of the century, weddings gowns took on a tailored look. . . . [Some] could have been based on conventional women's suit patterns, although their gala purpose dictated trimming that transformed them to something much more festive." In 1903, a "tight skirt, exaggerated bosom, tiny waist and leg-o'-mutton sleeves" were fashionable. Likewise, a wedding outfit from the early 1920s "reflects the transitory fashion of the period to a greater degree than many of our traditional wedding gowns today."

— Wedding Album

Though not as varied as styles, brides had had (or taken) some leeway in the color of their gowns in the late nineteenth century, although perhaps not with the approval of the doyennes of etiquette. White had not always been the rule for even the most fashionable weddings, but in the nineteenth century it swept both the United States and England in both popularity and correctness. By the 1870s, white had "truly caught on," writes Ann Monsarrat. "In 1840, Mary Stanley Bunce Dana wrote (in *Passing under the Rod*): 'I saw the young bride in her beauty and pride,/Bedecked in her snowy array' and the same could have been said by guests at virtually all high society and middle class weddings on both sides of the Atlantic from 1820 on. Even the horses which pulled the bride to the church were now white."

Even so, not everyone did wear white. For example, Maud Burke wore gray for her wedding to Sir Bache Cunard in New York in 1895. And by the late 1920s even the doyennes began to change their guidelines for correctness in the color of wedding gowns in polite society, although white remained the most popular choice.

THE BRIDE'S COSTUME

The Wedding Gown—"There is," said Douglas Jerrold, "something about a wedding gown prettier than any other gown in the world."

And this is true whether the bride glitters in wondrous satin or is demure in a simple organdie. Something of the hallowed customs and forms and traditions connected with this ever-old and ever-new ceremony seems to glorify this gown and to imbue it with a mystic loveliness.

Materials for the Formal Gown

Shimmering satin—"wedding satin" it is sometimes called—is our vision when we think of the formal wedding dress, for traditionally, in song and story, the bride dresses in satin. For the handsome, important wedding gown, wedding satin, with its elegance, its dignity, its grace and stateliness, is the Queen of Fabrics. Formerly, and sometimes now, wedding satin was of a heavy, stand-by-itself quality, a quality reflected perhaps in the old heavy wedding rings. But now usually the satin that is used to fashion the bridal gown is soft in texture, graciously adaptable in its folds, supple rather than heavy.

For the regal bride who wishes an alternative to satin, but an alternative fully as formal in its registry, there is panne or chiffon or transparent velvet in white, or more softly lustrous, in ivory tone. This velvet dress is, of course, limited in its season, as are those other materials appropriate to the elegant bride, white moire, plain or exquisitely metalized, silver lamé, and rich silver and gold tissue or brocade.

Other materials—staple materials—appropriate for the formally dressed bride are satin crêpes and silk crêpes. Satin crêpes are very satisfactory, very soft, and so are *crêpe de Chine* and the other silk crêpes which from year to year vary as to texture as they vary in name. Lace—delicate, shadowy—is always lovely—and so is georgette. And then—especially appropriate for the young and slender bride—there are soft, lustrous taffetas and flattering chiffons and billowy tulles or nets. All of these materials are appropriate "the year 'round."

Color

Traditionally and conventionally the wedding gown is white, because of the religious quality associated with white, because of the symbolism of white, and because of its association with youthful simplicity and charm.

This tradition of white includes, of course, the creams—light and dark—and the tones of ivory and "old ivory."

The first touch of color in the wedding gown—and it was regarded indeed as a rebel against tradition—was the introduction of the faintest tint of flesh, rose, or light blue, in the lining or facing of the wedding gown of heavy white satin or velvet, or in the folds of chiffon that lined the train or in the bands of pearl embroidery at the hem.

This slight touch of a tint in the lining of the wedding dress or train became even more a rebel, in 1925, under the sponsorship of Captain Molyneux, who in some of his creations, departed from the traditionally-accepted wedding gown of white to the gown of pastel tints, notably blush rose.

So now, besides the traditional white and ivory, the bride may for her formal wedding gown, choose a blush rose or a gown of silver cloth or even of gold.

Type

For the mode of her wedding dress the bride has a wide choice—from the picturesquely beautiful period gown, to the modernistic gown which quickly reflects the prevailing fashions in styles.

As a general rule, no matter what the type of bride and her attendants, the period gown gives to the wedding picture a sense of peculiarly appropriate beauty, of romance.

However, if the bride considers that she is not the "type" to wear a robe of history, or if she is a very modern-minded person with a very modern taste, or if she must plan to have the dress serve later as an evening dress or dinner dress, she will probably choose a smart

modern day or evening mode, modified or embellished to suit her taste.

Sleeves

Although there is no definite rule about sleeves, the long close-fitting or tight sleeve seems always the most popular. And quite deservedly so, for it withstands most successfully the perspective at which a wedding gown is usually viewed. However, some types of dresses have half-sleeves, and some have no sleeves at all. For the evening, wedding gowns sometimes have sleeves of lace. The sleeves in the wedding gown may, like the train, be removable.

Embellishments

Although the formality of the wedding gown is indicated by its mode rather than by its adornment, the wedding gown may be, if the bride chooses, embroidered in silver, in pearls, in crystals. Seed pearls are always especially popular for the embroidery of wedding gowns, and perhaps one reason is that often they reflect a soft radiance from the church lighting.

Lace, precious lace from the family treasure-chest, "heirloom lace," or newly-bought lace, has always been considered a "lucky sign" as a decoration for a wedding costume—and indeed it should be. The lace—rose point usually—may be simply or lavishly used, for dress-trimming, or veil or cap or train. Heirloom lace harmonizes especially well, of course, with a period costume. The lace should not be cut.

The Train

Whether the train is short or medium or of the stately length prescribed for "court" trains, depends on the style of the dress and the preference of the bride.

And on the style of the dress too depends whether the train is attached to the shoulder or to the waist. In either case, it is attached in such a way that it can be removed after the wedding.

Sometimes there is a train of gleaming satin or of the dress-material and sometimes a tulle train over which falls the long, full veil of tulle.

—Weddings: Modes, Manners and Customs

Brides who preferred an informal wedding to a formal one were nonetheless expected to be dressed in perfect taste. An approved alternative to the formal wedding gown was the *traveling dress*.

A WOMAN is sometimes married in what is called a travelling dress, but the term is usually a misnomer. This attire, as a rule, is a visiting gown, with bonnet or hat, and gloves that are in harmony. Of course this toilet is exchanged as soon as possible for a less noticeable and expensive one.

Black is not a suitable color for any bride to wear at her marriage. Superstition should not influence any one in any matter, but black has a sombre effect on the spirits. Even where marriages occur soon after the saddest of events, there is always a simple white gown that is entirely appropriate for any woman's garb, if she is still young enough to marry, and no woman was ever too old for that.

For this ceremony, which is, or ought to be, a religious one, white is very properly assumed under any circumstances. Good form approves this, even where crape is assumed an hour afterwards.

—Weddings Formal and Informal

By the 1920s, "traveling dress" did mean a dress in which one would travel.

IF a bride chooses to be married in traveling dress, she has no bridesmaids, though she often has a maid of honor. A "traveling" dress is either "tailor made" if she is going directly on a boat or train, or a morning or afternoon dress—whatever she would "wear away" after a big wedding.

—*Etiquette*

Other options included:

WHEN the bride wishes to indicate that her wedding is to be *informal*, she plans to wear informal clothes: she may wear a white dress, but with no train, and, instead of a veil, she wears a hat. Or instead of wearing a white dress, she may wear an afternoon dress of some becoming light shade, and a picturesque hat, say of horsehair or velvet. Or she may wear a simple of elaborate silk ensemble or an ensemble of a heavier textile, or, most informally, a traveling suit. . . .

Or perhaps—and many a bride has had to face this problem—she and her fiancé are bravely starting life together with a very small income, too small for the groom to stretch his budget to buy the formal clothes which would be demanded if the bride wore the traditional white wedding dress and bridal veil, and which in the simple life that they are to lead in the small place where they are to make their home for at least some years to come, he would have no occasion to wear. Sad it is, but necessary, the bride must, in this exigency, readjust her plans to wear the dress of a "real bride," (with white dress and train and veil), and wear the informal costume more in keeping with the business suit that the groom and his best man will wear.

As for her dress it may be of the afternoon type or of the traveling type appropriate to her wedding-plans. If,

for instance, she is planning to have a simple house wedding and does not wish to wear bridal white, she might wear a dress of crêpe satin or silk crêpe (such as crêpe de Chine), georgette, chiffon, taffeta, or, in summer, organdie. And a lace dress is always most effective for this kind of wedding.

The shade of this informal dress will be a "favorite" shade, one that the bride knows is especially becoming to her. Flower shades, especially those in fashion in the season in which she is being married, are often chosen.

And in planning this informal costume, the bride has a really more difficult problem than the bride who plans a formal wedding gown, for, whereas the formally dressed bride follows certain traditions in her costume, the informally dressed bride must be most careful that what she plans to wear is, although informal, in perfect and appropriate taste.

If the bride decides to wear such informal attire, she will dispense with a procession and will undoubtedly decide to have no attendants or only one attendant. And this attendant will dress in the same general mode.

The informally dressed bride may carry a shower bouquet, if she wishes, but usually she prefers to carry a small bouquet, a Colonial bouquet, for instance. With a suit she usually finds it more convenient and appropriate to wear a corsage bouquet.

If the ceremony takes place as early as nine o'clock in the morning, a severely simple traveling costume would be worn by the bride if the couple are to start immediately afterwards on the honeymoon.

If the bride goes to the clergyman's house or the parish house to be married, it would seem most consistent and appropriate for her to wear a street costume and a hat.

—Weddings: Modes, Manners and Customs

ACCESSORIES

Having chosen the most appropriate dress for her particular wedding and her own tastes, a bride needed to consider the following accessories:

The Wedding Veil

"TRAILING clouds of glory"—the wedding veil. The dream-like mists of billowy tulle, voluminous, ethereal. The regal cascade of wondrous old lace. Flattering tulle, lace-edged. Exquisite lace, gracefully draped over tulle. Lovely tinted sunrise clouds of blush-rose. Whichever type the bride chooses, it should crown the wedding dress with an aura of loveliness and mystery.

Delicate orange blossoms usually are given the exquisite duty of "holding in place" the wedding veil—a group of tiny drooping blossoms over each ear, or a slender bandeau or wreath of orange blossoms, or even a tiara of orange blossoms for the stately bride.

Pearls too, in a half circle or a full circle, are often used as a bandeau.

The youthful pearl cap—the Juliet cap—the melon-shaped cap of tulle or lace, the cap smoothed across the forehead (and sometimes, with a nun-like effect, banded under the chin, disclosing only the face), a medieval headdress, a circlet or tiara of silver cloth combined with pearls or orange blossoms or closed buds, a lace coronet or tiara of the Russian or Oriental type—any of these may be chosen from the fashion panorama of the present or the past. But the type chosen must, of course, be of the same theme as the gown.

As wondrously lovely as a wedding veil inevitably is, beauty is not its only mission, for fundamentally it is the wedding veil that proclaims the standard of formality for the wedding. When the bride plans to wear a wedding veil, she indicates that her wedding is to be formal, and

when this significant detail is determined, all other details, to be consistent with this formality, assume a formal air. Especially is this true, of course, of the clothes of the groom and his attendants: *appropriate formality* will then be the standard of their clothes.

Gloves

About wearing gloves there is no definite rule. In some seasons almost all brides will wear gloves, and in the following season, one will rarely see gloves. Formerly wedding gloves were always white kid; of late long, soft, suede gloves seem more consistent with the softer satin materials.

In spite of changing customs, however, it would seem a reasonable rule for the bride to wear gloves, if the formality of her costume seems to demand them, if they complete the harmony of her costume.

Slippers

Like all other accessories, the bride's slippers depend on the type of her dress. Plain white or ivory satin pumps are usually worn, but her slippers may, if she wishes, be embroidered with seed pearls—especially effective if the dress is also pearl-embroidered—or they may have a pearl-embroidered buckle, or a rosette fashioned of tulle or lace and orange blossoms.

Her Handkerchief

The tiny handkerchief that the bride carries usually is a symbol of some lovely sentiment—it may be fashioned of rare old lace belonging to her mother or grandmother, or it may be a gossamer bit of hand-woven linen given her by a dear friend.

Jewels

Tradition and sentiment are expressed in the jewels that the bride wears on her wedding day. Her engagement-ring—usually a diamond but now often an emerald or sapphire or ruby or her birthstone—she wears during the ceremony, on her right hand. The wedding ring, sometimes still a plain circlet of gold, is usually now of platinum, plain or engraved or set with small brilliants, round or square-cut. And then the other "gift of the groom"—the traditional string of pearls, a bracelet, or brooch. Or "the gift of the bride's father" may be the string of pearls, if the groom gives her the bracelet or brooch.

The Bride's Bouquet

To fulfill their appealing mission of being the climax of the bridal costume, the flowers in the bride's bouquet seem to be lent an especial glory, a wonder of romance, a delicate mystery that proclaims their sweet importance. These eloquent ambassadors are too the expression of the time-honored privilege that the groom has of sending the bridal bouquet to his bride.

Whether the bridal bouquet is an exquisite cascade of the flowers traditionally appropriate for the shower bouquet, or an armful of her favorite roses, a spray of exotic white orchids, a delicate bouquet of lilies-of-the-valley, a sheaf of dignified calla lilies, or a gem-like corsage for the simpler wedding, it "seizes a beauty from the skies" and wears it triumphantly. Since the bridal bouquet must be in harmony with the bridal costume, the groom consults the bride as to her preferences, and interprets them as a devoted cavalier should and would do.

What flowers shall the bride carry? It depends on the style of the wedding gown and the formality of the wedding. If

the gown is in the ultra-fashion of the moment, a bouquet should be arranged to be consistent with the details of this fashion. If the gown is of a certain marked period, the flowers should then add the most distinguishing touch to the effect of that period. But above all, the flowers should be "becoming." That is, they should project the individuality of the wearer. One should feel, when seeing the bridal bouquet, an exquisite sense of completeness.

The shower bouquet, which is the conventional bridal bouquet, is one of the loveliest and most graceful arrangements for bridal flowers. This arrangement allows a luxuriant and massed effect in the arms of the bride, and, through tiny branches of small flowers tied at intervals to narrow streamers of white ribbons of varying lengths, it gives a lovely and interesting effect of artistic irregularity.

The flowers we usually associate with shower bouquets are orange blossoms, small white orchids, gardenias, roses, white azaleas, white jasmine, lilies-of-the-valley, white lilacs, white iris, white columbine, white sweet peas.

As the background for any of these combinations, the long tapering sprays of exquisite lilies-of-the-valley should lend their feathery grace. Sometimes the bride chooses to have only these ethereal valley-lilies in her bridal bouquet.

The Junoesque bride sometimes elects to carry a bouquet composed of flowers of a larger form than those which give a cloud-like effect. For this there are large orchids, pointed shell-like white rosebuds, and half-open roses, delicately modified perhaps with velvety white pansies or with white sweet peas.

Or, if the bride has chosen a medieval or other stately effect for her wedding, she may carry a sheaf of calla lilies or madonna lilies. If she carries calla lilies, no attempt should be made to soften their classic beauty with anything but their own green leaves, which should be the smallest of the young leaves. And it is a mistake to imagine that because the form of the calla lily is large,

only a few should be carried. As many should be carried as the height of the bride will artistically permit.

If the bride has selected a Colonial effect for her wedding, her bridal bouquet (and the bouquets also of her attendants) may be of the Colonial type, the demure bouquet composed of tight rows of small flowers circled about a central flower, the whole collared with a little frill of delicate lace paper or wired real lace. The central flower, for instance, may be a gardenia or a white rosebud or a tiny white orchid, and circling it may be alternating rows of white sweet peas or tiny branches of white lilacs or orange blossoms. This bouquet too has a shower effect, made by small bunches of flowers tied to varying lengths of white ribbon and falling gracefully from the white-satin-bound handle.

The Prayer-Book

Instead of a bouquet, the bride sometimes carries a prayer-book, covered with an ivory-toned cover to blend with her ivory satin, or with a piece of the white satin of her dress perhaps, or with white velvet to match a velvet dress. This is particularly effective for the classic bride. Sometimes cascading from the prayer-book are markers of narrow satin streamers clustered at intervals with lilies-of-the-valley or orange blossoms, and sometimes the gold clasp is engraved with the monogram of the bride and the date of the wedding.

—*Weddings: Modes, Manners and Customs*

And, for a wedding in cooler weather:

WHITE, of course, is the most suitable. White fur, white velvet, white matelassé (if in fashion)—in fact, any material

in white which the mode approves. Silver cloth might be possible, or silver and white, or gold and white brocade, if they were smart at the time. It has been suggested that any cloak selected at this time might be used for the evening wrap later.

—Vogue's Book of Brides

In this country, *veils* were not widely worn before the mid-1800s, although instances date back to the Revolutionary War era. In other parts of the world, brides had worn veils for centuries and for many different reasons, some or all of which may have affected American women's choice to adopt them.

As for her veil in its combination of lace or tulle and orange blossoms, perhaps it is copied from a head-dress of Egypt or China, or from the severe drapery of Rebecca herself, or proclaim the knowing touch of the Rue de la Paix. It may have a cap, like that of a lady in a French print, or fall in clouds of tulle from under a little wreath, such as might be worn by a child Queen of the May.

The origin of the bridal veil is an unsettled question.

Roman brides wore "yellow veils," and veils were used in the ancient Hebrew marriage ceremony. The veil as we use it may be a substitute for the flowing tresses which in old times fell like a mantle modestly concealing the bride's face and form; or it may be an amplification of the veil which medieval fashion added to every head-dress.

In olden days the garland rather than the veil seems to have been of greatest importance. The garland was the "coronet of the good girl," and her right to wear it was her inalienable attribute of virtue.

Very old books speak of three ornaments that every virtuous bride must wear, "a ring on her finger, a brooch on her breast and a garland on her head."

A bride who had no dowry of gold was said nevertheless to bring her husband great treasure, if she brought him a garland—in other words, a virtuous wife.

At present the veil is usually mounted by a milliner on a made foundation, so that it need merely be put on—but every young girl has an idea of how she personally wants her wedding veil and may choose rather to put it together herself or have it done by some particular friend, whose taste and skill she especially admires.

If she chooses to wear a veil over her face up the aisle and during the ceremony, the front veil is always a short separate piece about a yard square, gathered on an invisible band, and pinned with a hair pin at either side, after the long veil is arranged. It is taken off by the maid of honor when she gives back the bride's bouquet at the conclusion of the ceremony.

The face veil is a rather old-fashioned custom, and is appropriate only for a very young bride of a demure type; the tradition being that a maiden is too shy to face a congregation unveiled, and shows her face only when she is a married woman.

—Etiquette

ℬ ℬ ℬ

A WEDDING veil may be from three to five yards long, and the train underneath is of the same length. If no train is worn the veil is a trifle longer than the bride's dress, but should it be of lace it should not trail the floor unsupported by tulle or net.

—Vogue's Book of Brides

The wearing of *orange blossoms* on the veil, as a wreath, or on the gown was another tradition with ancient roots that surfaced in this

country in the 1800s. The blossoms are a fertility symbol and the custom is thought to have been introduced in Europe by either the Moors or the Crusaders, who found it practiced among the Saracens. More recently, the fashion may have started up in France. They were soon *de rigueur* here. Both fresh blossoms and wax ones were worn, and some hold the notion that they must be burned no later than one month after the wedding to avoid bad luck.

Some brides eschewed *gloves*, at least during the ceremony, for convenience:

> WITHIN a few months several brides, whose social positions in New York and Boston entitle them to the right of creating fashions, have worn no gloves at their marriages, but have assumed them for their receptions. There is a convenience in this plan that warrants its establishment as a permanent usage. The awkwardness of removing a glove, and replacing it at the altar, and the ugliness of having the ring finger loosely covered by a bit of ripped kid, ought to have earlier brought brides ungloved into churches.
>
> — *Weddings Formal and Informal*

Other brides were not daunted by "a bit of ripped kid," a couple of inches of the seam of the ring finger cut so that the finger could be exposed at the appointed moment to receive the ring and the glove then replaced for the rest of the ceremony.

No bridal ensemble would be complete, of course, without *something old, something new, something borrowed, and something blue* — and in the 1920s, "a lucky sixpence in your shoe" as well, as this vignette so vividly conveys:

> [E]VERYONE seemingly is in [the bride's] room, her mother, her grandmother, three aunts, two cousins, three bridesmaids, four small children, two friends, her maid, the dressmaker and an assistant. Every little while, the

parlor-maid brings a message or a package. Her father comes in and goes out at regular intervals, in sheer nervousness. The rest of the bridesmaids gradually appear and distract the attention of the audience so that the bride has moments of being allowed to dress undisturbed. At last even her veil is adjusted and all present gasp their approval: "How sweet!" "Dearest, you are too lovely!" and "Darling, how wonderful you look!"

"Oh, Mary," shouts someone, "what have you on that is

> **Something old, something new,**
> **Something borrowed, something blue,**
> **And a lucky sixpence in your shoe!**"

"Let me see," says the bride, "'old,' I have old lace; 'new,' I have lots of new! 'Borrowed,' and 'blue'?" A chorus of voices:

"Wear my ring," "Wear my pin," "Wear mine! It's blue!" and someone's pin which has a blue stone in it, is fastened on under the trimming of her dress and serves both needs. If the lucky sixpence (a dime will do) is produced, she must at least pay discomfort for her "luck."

—Etiquette

The Groom's Attire

Getting dressed for the wedding was, then as now, simpler for the men. Full proper attire could be summed up as follows:

Gentlemen's Dress

Day Weddings

GROOM and best man, Prince Albert or cutaway coat, light trousers, black vest. Ushers, same coat and vest, dark trousers.

Evening Weddings

Fine twilled black corkscrew, or black Thibit dress coat, silk faced to button-holes, edges bound narrow; vest same material, embroidered, or heavy white silk or satin, embroidered; trousers same material as coat with silk braid down the side. Groom, best man and ushers all alike.

Gents' Furnishing

Day Weddings

Standing collars with natural roll, white loose puff silk scarf, pearl colored gloves, narrow pearl stitching for groom and best man, and narrow black stitching for ushers.

Evening Weddings

Shirt with narrow row of embroidery down the edges of bosom, standing collar with natural roll, white lawn tie one and one quarter inches wide, square ends, pearl colored gloves, narrow pearl stitching for groom and best man, and black stitching for ushers.

— *Wedding Etiquette and Usages of Polite Society*

However, more complete details on male dressing etiquette were useful:

THE BRIDEGROOM'S CLOTHES FOR A FORMAL DAY WEDDING

FOR the formal day wedding, that is the wedding in which the bride wears the traditional white dress and bridal veil, and which takes place before six-thirty in the

evening, the groom, best man, and ushers wear formal day clothes. Here they are, in detail:

Coat: Cutaway (also called "morning coat"). Black or dark oxford gray.

Waistcoat: The waistcoat may be of the same material and the same color as the coat. Often the groom wears a white linen or piqué waistcoat.

Trousers: Dark striped trousers.

Shirt: White linen or piqué. Stiff bosom. Plain.

Tie: Three types of neckties are correct to wear with the cutaway:

1. The Ascot tie, which at present is the smartest tie for the groom and his attendants to wear with a cutaway. The Ascot may be plain gray, or gray and black, or black and white.
2. The bow-tie. Not all-white or all-black. Frequently polka dot.
3. The four-in-hand. Black and white, striped or figured. Gray.

Collar: With an Ascot or bow tie, the wing collar is worn, and with a four-in-hand tie, either a wing or turned-down collar may be worn.

Socks: Black silk.

Shoes: Black calfskin or patent leather oxfords.

Spats: Spats are optional. White linen spats are very smart for a spring or summer wedding.

Jewelry: Plain gold, or platinum, or mother-of-pearl links.

Gloves: Light gray suede or buckskin, or white doeskin.

Handkerchief: White linen.

Overcoat: Black or oxford gray Chesterfield, or dark overcoat.

Hat: Silk hat.

Walking-Stick: Of plain malacca or other dark wood, with a straight or crooked handle.

Boutonnière: A single white flower, a gardenia or carnation.

Muffler: White or gray or black silk.

There is no difference between the formal clothes worn at a formal morning wedding and those worn at a formal afternoon wedding.

ℱ℈ ℱ℈ ℱ℈

FOR the formal *evening* wedding, in church, house, or hotel, the groom, best man, and ushers wear full dress. This is, of course, in accordance with the formality that the bride has established when she decides to wear the traditional white dress and bridal veil. Dinner jackets (the so-called Tuxedo suit) are not correct.

Here are the details of full dress:

Coat: Tailcoat. Black worsted, dull finish.

Trousers: Of the same material as the coat (black worsted, dull finish.) The outer seam of the trousers should be braided.

Waistcoat: White linen or piqué, single or double breasted.

Shirt: Plain. White linen or piqué. Stiff bosom.

Collar: Wing.

Tie: Plain white linen or piqué bow tie.

Shoes: Patent leather.

Socks: Black silk.

Handkerchief: White linen.

Hat: Silk hat.

Gloves: White kid.

Overcoat: Chesterfield or dark overcoat. (An overcoat is worn with full dress even in summer.)

Jewelry: Pearl studs, mother-of-pearl, and platinum sets most in favor.

Walking Stick: Malacca or plain wood. Straight stick favored with evening wear.

Muffler: White silk.

Boutonnière (if any): White.

— *Weddings: Modes, Manners and Customs*

Ironically, in the nineteenth century, the attire for men for a formal daytime wedding was not viewed as being as formal as his bride's ensemble. However, his wearing evening dress at the "wrong" time of day was a worse *faux pas* than his diverging from his bride in degree of formality.

AT a ceremonious marriage the bride wears by day a full evening dress, but a groom and all men guests appear only in morning attire.

That custom should approve of a toilet of ceremonious elegance for the bride who is wedded before evening, and compel the groom to appear in garments that he would wear in making an informal morning call, is questionable taste. However, as many combined judgments have established our usages, this style of dress for men at weddings by day must be followed, whether individually approved or not.

Grooms, however independent, are not likely to choose their own wedding day, nor yet those of others, for a public rebellion against fashion. Indeed, no man with a delicate regard for the habits and opinions of fashionable and other well-clothed persons will ignore usages, and appear in any other attire than a morning dress, freshly and daintily gloved. This dress is a dark frock coat, with lighter waistcoat and trousers, or a coat and vest alike, and trousers of a lighter color, and a light necktie or scarf. Tan or light gray gloves are the present fashion and it never varies very much. Sometimes an entire suit of one color is worn, that concession being made to age or becomingness.

Of course, for evening weddings all men wear evening dress, even when brides are in travelling or visiting costume, and are bonneted.

—Weddings Formal and Informal

At an informal wedding, different clothing was appropriate:

THE sack suit, sometimes called a business suit, and sometimes a lounge suit, consists of the sack coat, trousers, and waistcoat, all matching. Dark blue and oxford gray are the best colors to wear at the informal wedding.

With this suit the accessories that should be worn are the accessories that should be worn on any other occasion with a sack suit. That is, the groom should not choose accessories that seem more festive—a white bow or four-in-hand tie, for instance, or a colored waistcoat or white socks or tan shoes, or gloves. He should wear a plain white shirt, a wing collar or a starched turned-down collar. A four-in-hand tie is usually most becoming and always most appropriate, not all-white or all-black, but of a conservative subdued color and pattern, one with a dark background and narrow white single or grouped stripes, for instance. His shoes should be black oxfords, and his socks of dark silk or wool or lisle. The cuff links are of a conservative style too, of gold or enamel. Scarf pins are now not often worn. The appropriate hat for this suit is the derby or soft felt, or a straw hat. No gloves are worn with the sack suit.

For the informal house wedding taking place after six-thirty or seven o'clock in the evening, the groom and the other men in the wedding party may wear full dress or they may substitute the informal dinner jackets, Tuxedo suits. *But the Tuxedo suit may be worn only when the bride dresses informally.* The Tuxedo suit, since it is evening wear, should not be worn before six-thirty or seven o'clock in the evening. Under no circumstances is it a substitute or alternative for the formal day clothes — although many men try to convince themselves that it is!

—*Weddings: Modes, Manners and Customs*

CHAPTER 6

The Attendants

𝕏

THE BRIDE'S ATTENDANTS

A fashionable bride had at least one bridesmaid, often more, and might also have pages and flower girls to attend her.

CHOOSING THE BRIDESMAIDS

THE bride may have as few or as many attendants as she chooses — she may have none, or she may be preceded down the aisle by a procession of ten bridesmaids, a maid of honor (and perhaps a matron of honor also), two flower girls, and, for good measure, have one or two little boys to "attend" her train. But it is the usual wedding in which there is not at least a maid of honor or a matron of honor.

In the average wedding now, there are four or six bridesmaids, besides the chief attendant, who is either a maid of honor or a matron of honor. If the chief attendant is married, she is referred to, conveniently, as the matron of honor. It is the custom for the bride to choose her sister as her maid or matron of honor, or, if she has no sister, her most intimate friend.

When the bride selects her attendants, she usually pays honor to the groom and his family by including among her bridesmaids a sister or cousin of the groom. Sometimes too she invites the groom's sister to be her maid of honor, but usually this place is dedicated to her own sister or the friend whom she has always thought of as attending her on her wedding day. The former dictum that the bridesmaids should be unmarried no longer holds, and now one sees weddings in which as many of the bridesmaids are married as are unmarried. Often all the bridesmaids are married, and it would seem suitable that, if this is the case, the bride should have a matron of honor rather than a maid of honor.

To balance the wedding-picture, the bride should have an even number of bridesmaids,—two, four, six, eight, ten. They should walk together, two by two, in both the processional and the recessional. It makes an unbalanced picture to see a bridesmaid walking alone, and besides, this takes away from the glory of the chief attendant, who should walk alone in both the processional and the recessional.

— Weddings: Modes, Manners and Customs

ఖ ఖ ఖ

OF course, a bride has her bridesmaid or maids in her mind, if she intends to have them, almost as soon as she thinks of her wedding; also her maid, or maids of honor. It is in equal good form to ask one or two, but a single maid of honor is most common, because few brides have more than one especially dear girl friend. A sister, large or small, is as often chosen for this pleasant service as a girl outside of the family. This maid of honor should be notified of the bride's preference as soon as the date of the marriage is settled. Bridesmaids are also early requested to confer this tribute of affection.

— Weddings Formal and Informal

A bride's mother would never serve as a bride's attendant. (The mother could give her daughter away, however, if there were no male relatives.)

BRIDESMAIDS' ATTIRE

A bride might select her attendants' dresses:

> AFTER she has planned her own wedding dress, the most important problem that the bride has is the determination of the most beautiful and interesting "background" for that dress, the perfect foil to bring out the perfection of its loveliness. For, in arranging the wedding procession, it will be well to remember that although the social reason for having bridesmaids is the desire of the bride that she shall be attended by her friends, the artistic presentation requires that the attendants, like the lesser jewels of a perfect setting, should enhance the prominence and the beauty of the perfect gem.
>
> The attendants of the bride usually pay for their costumes. Sometimes the bride of wealth—and generosity!—supplies the costumes of her attendants, but usually the expense of the dresses of six or eight attendants is too much for the purse of the family already burdened by the thousand and one expenses of a wedding.
>
> But whether or not the bride furnishes the bridesmaid's dresses, she it is who decrees every detail of the costume. Then she instructs the bridesmaids as to her plans. And it is the first duty of every attendant to coöperate completely and heartily with the bride's directions as to the carrying out of every detail.
>
> The considerate bride will, of course, make every effort to make as light as possible the financial burden that she is perforce requiring of her attendants.
>
> —*Weddings: Modes, Manners and Customs*

Or, a bride might leave the choice of costume up to the bridesmaids themselves:

> HAVING accepted this honor, a bridesmaid is bound in honor to omit nothing reasonably proper, in effort or expense, to make the marriage of her friend an occasion of beauty and happiness. If the bride does not present her with a toilet for the occasion (and she seldom does unless she is exceptionally rich in comparison with her bridesmaids), she inquires of the bride in what gown she would be pleased to see her bridesmaids arrayed at her marriage, and complies exactly with her wishes. Of course, no considerate bride will lay a burden of serious expense upon any girl. As a rule, having given to each bridesmaid the names and addresses of the other bridesmaids, she refers them to each other, and asks them to agree among themselves what toilets will be pleasing to themselves.
>
> Wedding garments are of as much importance to the bridesmaids as they are to the bride.
>
> — *Weddings Formal and Informal*

The considerations entailed in attendants' attire were as numerous and complex as those for the bride's ensemble.

> THE dresses of the bridesmaids are of the same design and of the same material, although they may be of different colors. Usually too the dress of the maid of honor is of the same design as the dresses of the bridesmaids but almost always in her dress the colors are reversed, or the color may be quite different.
>
> The accessories of the costumes—slippers, stockings, gloves, hats, and bouquets—are also planned by the bride, since they must match or harmonize with the dress. The attendants' bouquets or any substitute for a bouquet— fans or chiffon muffs, for instance—are supplied by the bride, and sometimes too she gives her attendants their hats or slippers and stockings.

Sometimes the groom asks his bride for the privilege of sending the bouquets to her attendants, and in that case she usually goes with him to the florist's when the flowers are ordered so that the bouquets will be made as she has planned, to harmonize with the costumes and the decorations of the church and home. Under no circumstances, however, should any one of these bouquets be sent by the best man or any of the ushers.

The Color-Scheme

First the bride must decide the color scheme of her wedding. Then she decides whether she is to use that color exclusively, or shades of that color, or to combine that color with other harmonizing colors. This means a development of, or at least an appreciation of, a color-consciousness, so that she will be sure that her color-base is a beautiful and effective one, and that she will use variations of the same tone, never introducing an "off-tone" tint.

In a garden we often find the answer to the question — *What color should the bridesmaids wear?* Flower shades, delicate tints of every hue, are bridesmaids' colors: the exquisite blush-pink of a rose petal, the glowing yellow of a buttercup or daffodil, the delicate or lush greens that Nature so often uses for her backgrounds, periwinkle blue, the blue of the hydrangea or the deeper blue of the cornflower, the pink of the fuchsia or the hydrangea, the light or darker blues of the delphinium ("larkspur blue"), *bois de rose.*

Shades of pink—blush-pink, shell pink, peach, apricot— seem always lovely too in the frocks of the bridesmaids.

Then too there are the more sophisticated colors: the regal shade of the American Beauty rose, exotic orchid, mauve, deeper shades of green and deeper shades of rose, flame-color, turquoise blue, burnt orange, canary, maize, corn color, chartreuse, beige, cream, and silver or gold.

As in modes in general, every season shows certain shades in fashion. One year finds bridesmaids glowing in yellow, the next we see them looking very handsome in

green chartreuse (and a most lovely and interesting shade it is for weddings), this to be followed by a return to the exquisite youthfulness of shell-pink. One shade of green will be popular one season, while in the next season quite another shade will find favor.

When it is not the plan to have the details and accessories of the costume match, there are certain classic color-combinations that may be used: yellow or maize or corn-color with green (the different combinations often used by Nature herself), shades of green, of pink, shades of rose, shades of blue suggested perhaps by the different shades of delphiniums, combining shades of orchid, lavender, mauve and purple, the combination of pale yellow and burnt orange, amber dresses and yellow flowers.

For the rainbow wedding, pastel shades are used, of orchid, green and yellow, for instance, or shades of bluette, sea spray green and mauve, or blue, yellow and orchid, or pink, blue, yellow, and orchid. Or *composé* shades may be used, the bridesmaids in pale lavender, orchid, and violet, and the maid of honor in purple, or shades of pink and rose, from flesh pink, pale pink, deep pink, to the maid of honor in American Beauty rose. It is helpful to arrange different shades of sweet peas, to see how shades will combine and harmonize. The hats should be of exactly the same shade as the dresses.

The all-white wedding, with the bridesmaids in white instead of in pastel shades, and sometimes even wearing short white veils, is often lovely, but the effectiveness of such a wedding depends in great measure on the types of the bridesmaids. The all-white wedding needs very careful planning.

The Silhouette

The clever bride, with an eye for artistic line, will realize that a silhouette that might be most effective in the usual dress, may be distinctly ineffective for a dress that

must be viewed from the rather trying angles from which a processional-dress is observed. This is without a doubt one of the chief reasons for the renaissance of the period gown, the *robe de style*, the bouffant skirt and tight bodice, skirts with deep net or tulle scallops or hems, quaint berthas generous enough to form sleeves, lace fichus, round or pointed basques, skirts that hang longer in back than in front.

Materials

The materials of the dresses of the maid of honor and the bridesmaids? They vary, of course, from year to year, and they are more or less adapted to the season of the year. But despite changes there are the ever-popular and effective and practical family of crêpes, by whatever professional or picturesque name the current weaves are designated, adaptable georgettes, soft satins, graceful chiffons, youthful taffetas, summery organdies, picturesque (and expensive and perishable!) tulle, and combinations of lace over satin or georgette or other foundation of pastel shade, and the regal cloth of gold or cloth of silver.

Hats

"To match," "to harmonize," "to correspond," "to contrast"—these descriptive phrases offer us the best suggestions for the type of hat to be worn with the costumes of the attendants. Large, picturesque hats—of fine horsehair or transparent braid, of leghorn or Milan or Neapolitan straw, or of tulle or georgette or net or lace—are usually the most effective hats for the bridesmaids. In autumn and winter weddings, large velvet hats are much worn. Leaf brown velvet hats harmonize with many shades. Bridesmaids' hats usually have little trimming, their shape and materials forming their effectiveness. Picturesque effects are sometimes obtained with streamers.

Sometimes, instead of hats, the bridesmaids wear veils, silver veils with blue dresses, for instance, or lace veils with dresses of a medieval type.

With certain types of dresses, scarfs—of tulle or marines or net—are interesting.

—Weddings: Modes, Manners and Customs

Hats were worn at society weddings not only for reasons of fashion.

IN Roman Catholic churches and in most Ritualistic places of worship women cannot be present with uncovered heads; and it has become a general custom in consequence in all churches for bridesmaids to wear hats, bonnets, or short veils of tulle or gauze.

At home weddings bridesmaids very properly omit coverings for their heads, pretty as the effect of these decorations may be.

—Weddings Formal and Informal

To complete the costume of the properly dressed bridesmaid, slippers, gloves, and bouquets all had to be considered.

Slippers

IF the slippers and stockings are planned to match the costume, they should, to insure an exact match, be dyed to match a sample of the material.

Gloves

Bridesmaids now usually do not wear gloves, but it is correct for them to do so, if the bride considers that the harmony of their costumes would be served.

The Bridesmaids' Bouquets

The treatment of the attendants' bouquets, in color-conception and in form, should be most carefully planned, for the harmony of their costumes depends on this crowning touch.

For the spring wedding, gay, vari-colored spring flowers (jonquils, daffodils, narcissus, lilies-of-the-valley, and so forth), with perhaps one color predominating, are usually chosen, and for the autumn wedding, the mellow autumn colors, chrysanthemum shades or aster shades, are lovely.

There are certain flowers that are considered "background" flowers, flowers which felicitously combine with many different kinds of flowers—such as, the different shades of delphinium, snapdragon, narcissus, columbine, yellow roses.

Lately feathery African daisies, alone or in combination, have been extremely popular.

—Weddings: Modes, Manners and Customs

૪ૐ ૪ૐ ૪ૐ

COLONIAL bouquets, carried by the bride, bridesmaids, and flower girls are most effectively appropriate for the Colonial wedding.

Instead of bouquets the bridesmaids occasionally carry fans, and very occasionally chiffon muffs, but these, like shepherds' crooks, have, as a general rule, been discarded, since they are apt to give a garish, theatrical impression.

—Weddings Formal and Informal

With all of these adornments to purchase,

IF a bride is rich and her maids are less so, it is good taste to present them with gowns, hats, gloves, and shoes

for the wedding; but this is not obligatory, nor is it even a general custom. It is only a matter of personal preference and generosity.

— Weddings Formal and Informal

There were special considerations for the clothing of the maid or matron of honor:

THE dress of the maid of honor is usually of the same model as those worn by the bridesmaids—to maintain the uniformity and harmony of the picture-effect—although it usually is of a different shade. Her bouquet too is different in color and often in form.

— Weddings: Modes, Manners and Customs

💮 💮 💮

HER gown is generally more elegant in texture than that worn by bridesmaids. At present it is made with a demi-train, while bridesmaids' suits are no longer than their figures. If her toilette is not white, it should be of a pale tint, so that the bride may not seem to be too colorless in her wedding robes of white.

It is courtesy to consult the bride before selecting her gown, and she should be careful that its make or style should not lessen the bride's beauty, and that by the contrast of her own personality she does not detract from the charms of the young wife.

— Weddings Formal and Informal

ATTIRE FOR PAGES AND FLOWER GIRLS

THE costume of the diminutive flower girl or flower girls should take its cue from the extreme youth of the

young lady wearing it. It is not good taste to have the flower girl wear a sophisticated, and therefore inappropriate, frock. Her frock may be "quaint," of an old-fashioned type worn by children of a former age, of an alluring Kate Greenaway model, but it should never lay itself open to being classified as "grown-up." Here too appropriateness should be our keyword, and the simple charm of the little-girl personality, rather than the elaborateness of her costume, should be capitalized.

The frock may be a lovely soft white or delicately-shaded frock, say of shell-pink batiste or handkerchief linen—plain or exquisitely and simply embroidered—or an organdie or a plain or softly-pleated chiffon or georgette or perhaps a plainly-designed malines or very soft taffeta. Sometimes a ruffled dress or a petal-dress, if simply designed, is suitable.

It is logical too that the flower girl's frock should be of a rather plain model for it should serve as the simple background for the flowers from which she gets her designation. She may, with becoming simplicity, carry one lovely rose, or a small loosely-made bouquet of delicate pink sweetheart or butterfly rosebuds with perhaps a shower-effect made of tiny rosebuds attached to narrow flesh-colored ribbon streamers. Or in her arm she may hold a beautiful group of vari-colored Spring flowers. The flower-filled basket, too, we associate with a flower girl, and one sometimes sees the flower girl carry an engaging poke bonnet or an interesting and colorful French or Italian straw bag, plain or trimmed, filled with tiny-faced flowers, such as mignonette, rosebuds, pansies, forget-me-nots, lilies-of-the-valley. Sometimes in her basket or her picturesque straw bag, this little attendant carries rose leaves which in romantic fashion she scatters in the pathway of the bride and groom as they tread their lyric path down the aisle from the altar.

But the easiest bouquet for her to carry—and one almost always appropriate, and especially so with a long, quaint

frock in a high-waisted design—is the 1830 bouquet, a nosegay fashioned of rows of tightly-packed small flowers of pastel shades circled about a rose bud. These bouquets may be made with or without streamers.

—Weddings: Modes, Manners and Customs

In the nineteenth century, appropriate outfits for pages were

coats of green, red or blue velvet,—the two sometimes being unlike,—with white knee-breeches of satin and white silk hose. Perhaps garters with buckles are worn, also lace shoes with shining buckles of silver, steel or gold to correspond. Sometimes they wear hats of velvet to match their coats, each with a white plume, and a buckle very much like that upon their shoes, but ordinarily hats are omitted.

 da da da

ONE coat of emerald green and one of ruby, or one of sapphire blue and another of cardinal red, are effective combinations, and so also are two costumes of either one of these colors. Of course, hues worn by bridesmaids must not be repeated by them.

—Weddings Formal and Informal

The Little Lord Fauntleroy look was out of fashion by the late 1920s, however:

THE page or pages may wear dark or white suits with the long trousers and short plain Eton jackets, and a plain or ruffled Eton collar with a bow tie.

—Weddings: Modes, Manners and Customs

DUTIES OF THE BRIDE'S ATTENDANTS

THE bride's chief attendant is her maid of honor, usually called, if she is married, the matron of honor. She will make it her aim to be thoroughly coöperative with the wishes of the bride, carrying out in every possible way the plans of the bride that include her. Any other duties are on a purely social basis, and depend on the friendship of the bride and the maid of honor.

—Weddings: Modes, Manners and Customs

ﬔ ﬔ ﬔ

THE maid of honor stands next to the bride during the ceremony, also at the reception, and she goes with her to her room to assist her with her travelling attire. Here is also the privilege of casting a slipper after the departing carriage.

Whatever kindnesses the bride has been unable to express, where attentions were due, the maid of honor assumes during her absence, such as visiting elderly or invalid friends, or dependents, etc.

—Weddings Formal and Informal

At one time, aside from carrying out their roles in the ceremony faithfully and graciously, bridesmaids were expected to be extensions of the hostess at the wedding reception, and even to take on responsibilities in the days after the wedding.

AFTER the first half hour [at the reception] they see that guests are entertained by conversation, whether they have or have not been presented to them, and they are also alert to conduct timid women or girls to the refreshment room, whenever this part of the entertainment is

continuous and not a formal breakfast. If it is the latter, the mother of the bride or the hostess sees to this part of the festivity. They make themselves generally agreeable, it being bad manners for bridesmaids to allow themselves to be absorbed by one or two individuals whom they may happen to like.

Bridesmaids remain until after the departure of the bride and groom, grouping themselves in the hall or upon the porch, to wave their good ill, after an out-going daughter of the house. Sometimes it is arranged that a dance follows this departure, when the bridesmaids are rewarded for their self-denials while being agreeable to persons in whom they had no especial interest.

Bridesmaids should call upon the mother of a bride within a day or so after a wedding, when distance makes this considerateness possible. Sometimes it is arranged between the bridesmaids that one or more of them shall drop in daily at the house from which a daughter has gone forth, which is a very delicate courtesy. Whether or not they desire to show so much attention to a recent hostess, *good form* makes early and frequent visits to a mother from the dear friends of her daughter quite obligatory, or at least during the honeymoon, if it is spent away from home.

— Weddings Formal and Informal

More recently, bridesmaids could be more carefree—although they also became more exclusively decorative.

BESIDES generous and gracious coöperation with the decree of the bride as to carrying out the details of their costumes, the bridesmaids have not many duties, except to be prompt and helpful at the rehearsal, to be prompt and "pretty" at the wedding, and *to receive charmingly and graciously at the wedding reception.*

On the day of the wedding they meet at the bride's
house, collect their bouquets, and drive to the church in
the cars before the one containing the bride and her
father, who leave last.

—*Weddings: Modes, Manners and Customs*

The role of pages also evolved between the end of the nineteenth
century and the 1920s.

TWO little lads, dressed as court pages, frequently walk
behind the bride with the tips of her train in their hands.

These little fellows add much to the charm of groups at
the altar rail, and again at the reception they suggest gay
moving flowers, if they are graceful, well-bred lads.

The pages remove their hats on entering the church,
and as the bride kneels at the altar they lay down the
train. When the ceremony is completed, one standing on
each side of the aisle, they deftly lift the bride's train again
and carry it out of the church. These little accessories are
most likely to be added to the spectacle when there is only
a maid of honor, and no bridesmaids, but sometimes they
accompany a large retinue of marriage participants.

These little lads cannot be too thoroughly trained, and
certainly should be at the last rehearsal.

—*Weddings Formal and Informal*

✿ ✿ ✿

PAGES add a distinctly pretentious note to a wedding,
and are seldom seen, though to have them is in good taste,
if the bride wishes her wedding to have a regal touch.
Their duty is, of course, to hold the train of the bride, but
since the bridal train is usually of great beauty and since
its beauty if more effectively displayed as the train falls

naturally along the aisle, and since the bride usually is
so busy thinking of her own progress down the aisle,
she dispenses with any detail that even subconsciously
impedes that progress.

—Weddings: Modes, Manners and Customs

Flower girls always added a charming touch.

OF the children-attendants, flower girls are most effective and least pretentious. There may be one flower girl to
walk in single glory, or two flower girls to walk together,
either leading the processional, or, usually, between the
maid of honor and the bride. In the recessional, these
flower girls still walk together, usually before the bride
and groom.

—Weddings: Modes, Manners and Customs

The duties of the attendants of both bride and groom during the
wedding ceremony and reception will be described in Chapters 7 and 9.

GIFTS TO THE BRIDESMAIDS

THE bride's gift to her attendants is commemoration of
the happy event of her marriage may be a costly present, if
the bride is well-to-do, or it may be some modest remem-
brance, if the bride has to make a careful budget. Brides
often make a point of giving presents that may be worn by
the attendants on the day of the wedding, and these are, if
possible, monogrammed. Sometimes the date of the wedding and the intertwined initials of the surnames of the
bride and groom are engraved on them. In any event, usually the gift is a keepsake of an enduring nature.

A piece of jewelry to be worn at the wedding (bar-pin, brooch, pendant, etc.)

Necklace
Bracelet
Chain
Vanity case
Wrist Watch
Purse or handbag
Ear rings
Hair bandeau
Fan
Card case
Evening bag
Over-night bag
Gold key-ring
Powder case
Portfolio
Opera glasses
Pair of buckles
Jewel box
Short gold key-chain with gold tag for monogram
Gold or silver pencil or pen or both
Gold key in key case
Gold bill-clasp (monogrammed)
Traveling clock (gold, silver, enamel, or leather)
Fitted overnight bag, dressing-case, traveling-bag, or suit-case
Jeweled hat ornament
Monogrammed purse-mirror (gold or silver)

— *Weddings: Modes, Manners and Customs*

Also appropriate were a tulle muff (for winter weddings) or a parasol (for summer weddings) that coordinated with the bridesmaid's dress.

The Groom's Attendants

CHOOSING THE USHERS

At one time it was etiquette for a bride to have a say in the selection of male attendants.

> HOWEVER, it is more satisfactory when the friends and kinsfolk of the two families are not familiarly known to each other and are thrown together at a festivity, if one or more of the ushers are selected from the intimate friends of the groom's household, and the bride is discreet who is not too strenuous in maintaining her bridal prerogative in the selection of her ushers from among her own friends.
>
> — *Weddings Formal and Informal*

Although practices had changed by the 1920s, the idea that the bride's choices of attendants should affect the groom's lingered enough to prompt one arbiter of wedding etiquette to make this impassioned case against it:

> FROM time immemorial it has been customary for the groom to invite his brother to be his best man, just as it has been customary for the bride to ask her sister to be her maid of honor. If the groom has no brother, he asks his best friend.
>
> And may I say a word here parenthetically about the argument that sometimes divides families and, at least for the time being, causes much unfriendly feeling; that is, the question as to whether the groom should necessarily ask to be his best man the husband of the friend who has been invited by the bride to be her chief attendant or even one of the bridesmaids. It is absolutely not necessary for him to do this. It is absurd for married couples to take it for granted that they should both be asked to take part in a wedding party. Why should they be? It is possible that

the wife may be the bride's best friend and the husband be practically unknown to the groom. Therefore, why should he invite a stranger to be his attendant, an honor that naturally and consistently he wishes to give to his brother or best friend? A husband should not be expected to be invited to be an attendant just because his wife has been asked, or vice versa.

Another question that is often asked in this connection is: Is it correct to have married people as attendants? The answer is: Yes. Nowadays no distinction is made between married or unmarried people as attendants. Indeed now it is very much "done" to have several of one's young married friends in the wedding party.

— Weddings: Modes, Manners and Customs

The groom should take the following into account in selecting his attendants:

THE number of ushers for a church wedding is in proportion to the size of the church and the number of guests invited. At a house wedding there need be no ushers, since there usually are no duties for them, but it is correct to have ushers, honorary ushers, if the couple wish.

Since the ushers should walk together, two by two, in both the processional and recessional, the groom should invite an even number. As a compliment to his bride, the groom invites a brother of the bride or a favorite cousin, if she has no brother. The ushers may be married or unmarried men.

— Weddings: Modes, Manners and Customs

USHERS' AND BEST MAN'S ATTIRE

THE boutonnières worn by the men of the wedding party are usually of white, a single flower, a gardenia or a

carnation. Sometimes the groom adds to his flower a spray or two of lilies-of-the-valley from his bride's bouquet. Often the groom and his best man wear a gardenia, and the ushers wear carnations.

The groom furnishes these boutonnières for his attendants, and they are usually sent to the church to be claimed by the best man and ushers when they arrive. . . .

The best man wears exactly the type of clothes that the groom wears, with perhaps the exception of the boutonnière, the groom's often being more elaborate.

Occasionally too the ties of the groom and his best man differ from those worn by the ushers; the groom and best man, for instance, wearing ascots, and the ushers wearing four-in-hands.

The ushers, like the best man, wear the same type of clothes that the groom wears. However, . . . sometimes they wear waistcoats of the same material as their cutaways while the bridegroom and best man wear white waistcoats, and sometimes their boutonnières are a bit simpler. The groom, realizing the value of smart uniformity, will give them explicit directions as to what they are expected to wear, and he will send their ties and gloves to their homes, and their boutonnières to the church.

—*Weddings: Modes, Manners and Customs*

DUTIES OF THE BEST MAN

Best Man as Expressman

No one is busier than the best man on the day of the wedding. His official position is a cross between trained nurse, valet, general manager and keeper.

Bright and early in the morning he hurries to the house of the groom, generally before the latter is up. Very likely they breakfast together, in any event, he takes the groom in charge precisely as might a guardian. He takes

note of his patient's general condition; if he is "up in the air" or "nervous" the best man must bring him to earth and jolly him along as best he can.

His first actual duty is that of packer and expressman; he must see that everything necessary for the journey is packed, and that the groom does not absent-mindedly put the furnishings of his room in his valise and leave his belongings hanging in the closet. He must see that the clothes the groom is to "wear away" are put into a special bag to be taken to the house of the bride (where he, as well as she, must change from wedding into traveling clothes). The best man becomes expressman if the first stage of the wedding journey is to be to a hotel in town. He puts all the groom's luggage into his own car or a taxi, drives to the bride's house, carries the bag with the groom's traveling suit in it to the room set aside for his use—usually the dressing-room of the bride's father or the bedroom of her brother. He then collects, according to prearrangement, the luggage of the bride and drives with the entire equipment of both bride and groom to the hotel where rooms have already been arranged, sees it all into the rooms, and makes sure that everything is as it should be. If he is very thoughtful, he may himself put flowers about the rooms. He also registers for the newly-weds, takes the room key, returns to the house of the groom, gives him the key and assures him that everything at the hotel is in readiness. This maneuver allows the young couple when they arrive to go quietly to their rooms without attracting the notice of anyone, as would be the case if they arrived with baggage and were conspicuously shown the way by a bell-boy whose manner unmistakably proclaims "Bride and Groom!"

Best Man as Valet

His next day is that of valet. He must see that the groom is dressed and ready early, and plaster him up if he cuts himself shaving. If he is wise in his day he even

provides a small bottle of adrenaline for just such an accident, so that plaster is unnecessary and that the groom may be whole. He may need to find his collar button or even to point out the "missing" clothes that are lying in full view. He must also be sure to ask for the wedding ring and the clergyman's fee, and put them in his own waistcoat pocket. A very careful best man carries a duplicate ring, in case of one being lost during the ceremony.

Best Man as Companion-in-Ordinary

With the bride's and groom's luggage properly bestowed, the ring and fee in his pocket, the groom's traveling clothes at the bride's house, the groom in complete wedding attire, and himself also ready, the best man has nothing further to do but be gentleman-in-waiting to the groom until it is time to escort him to the church, where he becomes chief of staff.

—Etiquette

GIFTS TO THE USHERS

Views on what made appropriate gifts for the ushers, as well as how customarily they were bestowed, changed with the times, as they still do. In the nineteenth century,

IF the groom presents his ushers and best man each with a souvenir of his marriage, it is left by their plates [at the bachelor dinner]. Scarf pins are usual gifts—if any are bestowed—and these are likely to be thrust through the location or table card of each guest. Sometimes it is in the boutonnière that is laid at each plate.

—Weddings Formal and Informal

As the 1920s drew to a close, we find that the groom's

gift depends entirely upon the dress customs of the hour. A few years ago a scarf pin was the popular gift to ushers. As this book goes to press men are not wearing stick pins, but studs and cuff links of elegant design are chosen by grooms who have large incomes. Others give trifles like gold mounted fountain pens or pencils, belt buckles, key chains and key rings in sterling silver, cigarette and card cases.

— The Bride's Book of Etiquette

A more complete list suggested:

The following are appropriate gifts for the bridegroom to give to his best man and ushers:

Watch chain
Gold bill-clasp
Gold key-ring
Single pearl stud
Walking stick
Cigarette holder
Scarf-pin
Card-case
Wallet
Cigarette case — gold, silver, leather
Pocket watch or wrist watch
Gold or silver pencil
Gold or silver fountain pen
Gold or silver knife
Cuff links (Sometimes these links have the initials of the bridegroom on one half and the initials of the recipient on the other.)

Cigarette lighter
Short gold key-chain with gold tag for the monogram
Gold key-case and key
Long silver key chain
Match case, silver or gold
Black moire silk "evening set" consisting of cigarette-case, match-case, wallet

Sometimes the groom makes a distinction between the presents that he gives his best man and those he gives his ushers. Since the best man holds the position of greater honor in the wedding party, he is often given a handsomer or more considerable present. The gifts are usually given to the attendants at the bachelor dinner which the groom gives to his attendants, but at any rate, they are given at some time before the wedding.

Also the groom usually provides the tie, gloves, and boutonnières for his best man and ushers, and often their collars and spats. He usually sends the tie and the gloves to their homes, and the boutonnières are sent to the church where the best man and ushers receive them.

—*Weddings: Modes, Manners and Customs*

CHAPTER 7

A Church Wedding

Then as now, the centerpiece of "the great day" was the wedding ceremony itself. In polite society, church was almost always the venue for the utmost in formality of ceremony, as well as lavishness and expense, although it was also perfectly correct to have a simple church wedding or, provided one had the means, an elaborate wedding at home.

AN OVERVIEW

High excitement, bustle, and solemnity all rolled into one brief morning—here is a glimpse into what one might expect at a classic church wedding in our grandparents' day.

The Story of Formal Morning Wedding

THE formal wedding in all its glory may seem to verge in some respects into the class of the pageant, but those who have a natural preference for the grand manner in all things will want such an important event as a wedding in the family to be carried off with an air. And if the young couple and the bride's family are willing—though perhaps we should say that the groom is resigned rather than

willing—there is no reason why such tastes should not be indulged, and certainly the whole ceremony is made a delight to the onlooker.

Let us suppose then that the Van Gards' second daughter, Katrina, after a successful and happy launching a season or two ago, is to marry the oldest son of another of the town's important families. Katrina wishes to realize her youthful dreams regarding her wedding, the two families beam approval, and the plans are accordingly laid with a nice eye to detail. When the great day arrives, in November, there is a minimum amount of flurry and scramble, and the bride is surprisingly fresh looking after her round of parties and dressmakers. As for the groom, he is no more nervous than the average, and fortunately for him the best man is a miraculous mixture of the Rock of Gibraltar, a universal provider, and a devoted nurse.

High noon is the hour chosen for the ceremony, which is to take place at St. Botolph's, whose Gothic proportions need no embellishment in the way of flowers. The rector of St. Botolph's is to perform the ceremony, but the groom's great-uncle, a white-haired old bishop, is to pronounce the final blessing. And the vested choir, ranging from bright-eyed little boys in Eton collars to lanky basses, is to sing softly before the arrival of the bridal party.

Of course, the guests begin arriving early, particularly those eager ladies who all demand seats on the aisle, so that the diplomacy of the overworked ushers is sorely tried. These young men who, by some miracle of management had reached the church in plenty of time, although they had all been soundly sleeping at ten-thirty, are wearing black morning coats, black and white striped worsted trousers, wing collars, with black and white striped ties, and white waistcoats. Their boutonnières are gardenias.

The groom and best man are dressed like the ushers, except that the groom wears a pale gray Ascot tie and the best man one in a darker gray.

Thanks to tactful efforts seats are found for all the fortunate bearers of the engraved cards saying:

Please present this card
at St. Botoloph's Church
on Wednesday, the twenty-first of November

And a commanding position is found for even the little seamstress who has sewed for the Van Gards for the last twenty years, and who sits breathlessly waiting the dear child's appearance.

Finally, the groom's family are escorted to their place on the right; then the bride's on the left, and after the usual expectant sigh, the strains of *Lohengrin* herald the bridal procession. First come the ushers, two by two, and then the six bridesmaids, also walking in pairs. Katrina is devoted to both her sisters, and, since she could not have two maids of honour, has had none. The two Van Gard girls and four of Katrina's dearest friends are dressed alike in frocks of white crêpe roma, quite simply made, with long tight sleeves and a slight drapery on the left side to add to the formal character of the dress. They wear little close-fitting turbans of white pansies and carry white orchids. The bride's presents, brooches of crystal and marcasite, are pinned proudly on the shoulders of their frocks.

Of course, the bridesmaids look charming, but simply nothing in comparison with the bride, who is appropriately radiant as she comes up the aisle on her father's arm. Her dress of white velvet is made on classic lines, with a slim bodice, long, tight sleeves, and a long train. Her lace veil is one that her mother and grandmother wore before her, and she carries white orchids. To simplify matters, she has not worn gloves, and her engagement ring, a marquise diamond, adorns her right hand for the time being.

The groom and best man come in from the vestry and take their places at the right of the altar with the bride at

the left, and the bridesmaids and ushers divide into two groups on either side. And the bride's father, after making his proper responses, with just a suspicion of huskiness, slips into the pew by his wife, thankful that his part is played.

The actual ceremony over, there is the return procession, with everyone beaming; and the bride and groom, the attendants, and the notable guests are all confronted by a battery of photographers outside the church. This ordeal is ended, however, by the departure of the bridal party for the Van Gard house, and the final tangle of motors is straightened out with not too much waiting and backfiring.

—Vogue's Book of Brides

How a ceremony such as Katrina Van Gard's was planned and carried out is the subject of the rest of this chapter.

CHOICE OF CHURCH AND CLERGYMAN

In the Victorian era, women were considered to have, in general, a closer involvement in religious life than did men, and to have special rights or interests in all details of the wedding, yet a wife was also expected to defer to her husband in all important decisions. Deciding proper etiquette in case of a disagreement between the two was thus a bit of a juggling act.

A PAIR to be wedded may agree between themselves what music shall be performed, also what clergyman shall officiate, if they choose, but etiquette and long established custom gives to the bride the sole right in this matter, if she prefers to maintain it. The same supreme authority directs that the marriage be in the church attended by the bride's family, provided there is a church service. It would

be just as improper for a bride to be married in another's house as in a sanctuary not her own. Only exceptional circumstances justify a breaking of this social law. Chivalry, as well as justice, demands concessions from men to women in religious matters, provided the latter have strong feelings regarding the same.

If a bride has no fixed feeling about creeds, and the groom has, she yields after marriage to his sentiments and to his order of church going, but before marriage, and on the wedding day, the dignity of her family, also harmony, requires that she go to her husband from her habitual house of worship.

If a man cannot make this concession to his *fiancée*, he is likely to prove an arbitrary husband that only an angel could wed with safety.

It is a pretty custom, although not an invariable one, for the young woman to ask her pastor by note or verbally, to perform the marriage rite for her. This is a gratification to him, and he takes an early occasion to call upon her to inquire if she has any special ideals for administering marriage vows that he can properly comply with. Sometimes, of course, the bride's parents secure the clergyman's services.

— Weddings Formal and Informal

After the social upheavals of the decades following, the affianced apparently could expect a smoother resolution of this important question:

As a rule the wedding ceremony is performed in the church which the bride's family attends, or by her own clergyman if the ceremony is performed at home. If, however, the groom feels deeply on the subject, or if the bride expects to attend his church after her marriage, his clergyman may be invited to perform the entire ceremony, or to assist the bride's pastor. Again, if either the bride or groom counts a clergyman among relatives or intimate friends, he

may be invited to perform or assist in the ceremony. This is settled amicably by the bridal couple and their families.

— The Bride's Book of Etiquette

Once church and officiary were chosen, these practical matters needed to be addressed according to proper form:

> THE amount of the [clergyman's] fee varies from five dollars to one hundred, according to the means of the groom. The money or check is placed in an envelope and handed to the clergyman by the best man. If the ceremony is performed in a church the clergyman receives the fee in the vestry room, either immediately before or after the ceremony. At a home wedding the best man hands the clergyman the envelope just before he leaves.
>
> The clergyman should be consulted [before] plans for the wedding are discussed, never after invitations are issued. He may be leaving the city, or he may have been engaged for the same day and hour by another parishioner.
>
> The sexton of the church is paid a fee by the bride's parents which covers not only his services, but those of his attendants, and the heating and lighting of the church.

— The Bride's Book of Etiquette

And while it would have been only natural for a couple to choose a church of which either one or both were already members, there was a financial consideration as well:

> THE opening of the church, lighting, heating, sexton's attendance, organist, and incidental expenses may all be charged for to strangers. But it is not usual to charge for opening, lighting or heating, to people who own pews and belong to the congregation.

— Vogue's Book of Brides

For the clergyman's services, churches did not actually charge a fee; however, custom had long since decreed that it was proper etiquette to give one, or sometimes a gift.

THE REHEARSAL

IF there is to be a marriage party, that is, a maid of honor, bridesmaids, and perhaps pages; also a best man and ushers, a rehearsal of the procession and its grouping at the altar is a necessity. Even if a wedding is to be at home, this cannot safely be omitted. This plan secures grace of action, and artistic harmony of position. Indeed rehearsals for a marriage tableau are as necessary for a beautiful arrangement of the bridal party, as a drill for military evolutions.

One rehearsal ought to be sufficient, but sometimes it is not. The bride plans the order of entrance, the distances each person or persons shall walk apart, the grouping at the altar, and the manner of departure.

She also selects the music, and it is an excellent plan to have this performed at the rehearsal. This should occur several days before the marriage, whenever such a date is practicable, because last hours at home are usually full of time-consuming obligations. Besides numbers of notes that must be written immediately, there are replies to congratulatory letters, that must be prompt, and there are many large and small cares of all sorts that cannot be avoided. An early rehearsal also removes from the bride's mind an apprehension about the most trying part of the service.

A bride should look neither worried nor wearied under her marriage veil; much less should she have a flurried manner, as if she had lately found no repose in which to breathe tranquilly. A disturbed expression of countenance or manner at a marriage is bad form, because, as a rule, forethought and reasonable management of the details of a wedding make mental disturbance wholly needless. Of

course, the mother, or next friend, of a bride bears all the burdens of preparation and the arrangement of these matters, whenever it is possible.

The bride fixes the time for a marriage rehearsal, always consulting the convenience of its participants.

Having first clearly arranged in her own mind her marriage formalities, secured the church and the organist, . . . she writes notes, informing each participant of the details of her plans and the date of a rehearsal. This usage provides each of her party with the means of learning all the parts to be assumed at the ceremony, so that when the rehearsal occurs few or no directions need be given at the church. Of course, no unseemly flippancy is possible on this occasion among well-bred or properly reverent persons. Hilarity attending a wedding is becoming elsewhere than in a house of worship.

—Weddings: Modes, Manners and Customs

Some in polite society held that the bride should not take part in the rehearsal herself, only observe it, with a friend standing in for her.

DECORATIONS

THE decorations for the church wedding should correspond to the size and general plan of the wedding. Elaborate and massive decorations for a small wedding party would be in very bad taste. On the other hand, the decorations for a large and fashionable wedding may be very simple, if such is the wish of the bride. For the large church wedding a certain number of pews at the front are reserved for the families of the bride and groom and for their most intimate friends. At the entrance to each of these pews the florist fastens a bouquet of flowers. White ribbons stretched across the aisle mark the last of the reserved pews. The chancel is massed with ferns and the

altar with flowers. The choir benches, lectern, and pulpit are draped with smilax, fine ferns, or wreaths of flowers. For spring and summer weddings white garden flowers, like narcissus and lilies-of-the-valley, daisies or marguerites, snapdragons, candytuft, and rambler roses, may be used effectively, also dog-wood, mountain laurel and the blossoms of fruit trees, apple, pear, peach and cherry. White dahlias and asters are handsome for September, while chrysanthemums, roses, and carnations are favorite flowers for fall and winter weddings. Colored flowers are sometimes used at church weddings, but green and white provide the best background for a bride. For a church wedding in the country, garden and field flowers are often used with good effect in spring and summer; autumn leaves in the fall.

— The Bride's Book of Etiquette

ଫ୍ଲ ଫ୍ଲ ଫ୍ଲ

As a general rule, if the bridesmaids' dresses are to be in the delicate pastel shades now so fashionable, the florist will use blossoms whose tones are deep but clear, in perfect harmony or in harmonious contrast with the delicate tints. But if the bridesmaids' dresses are to be of any vivid hue, like pure yellow or deep pink, the decorator will probably use white or very pale flowers, to keep the color accent where it belongs. The flowers on the altar should be white—calla lilies, madonna lilies, white orchids, gardenias, white narcissus—and they should always be at the sides of the cross, never under it.

If flowers are placed at the ends of the pews, or of the first few pews, or on every fourth pew, a few blossoms of large form are usually more effective than small flowers, but clusters of small flowers are sometimes used. Care should be taken to use flowers that do not fade quickly.

— Weddings: Modes, Manners and Customs

WEDDINGS may be as simple as a runaway match. The bride and groom, with their families, may go to church, come back, have luncheon, and saunter off quietly to their honeymoon; or weddings may be as elaborate as a court pageant, with a bridal procession of perfect scenic effect. And between these two there are a dozen degrees of different procedures. In subsequent chapters, the most important of these will be fully described. Here we are more occupied with certain preparations.

Decorations for the church, if these are desired, must be decided upon and talked over with the florist. Decorations for the house, if anything more than cut flowers is required, must also be arranged for. The bridesmaids' bouquets are sometimes ordered with the decorations and sometimes sent by the groom. If the bride has some special wish about their matching the decorations she generally orders them herself. The groom always sends the bridal bouquet, however.

Some churches are so architecturally beautiful that to deck them out with flowers seems belittling. Some, and particularly small country churches, are much improved by floral ornamentation. Wreathes, sheaves, hanging baskets, festoons, bowers of branches, are all appropriate to the decoration of simple churches. For great, grand churches laurel arches and fern palms are, at least, safer than timid colour effects. Magnificence, or almost nothing, is to be advised.

Awnings for church and house are used, either if the weather is uncertain or if the event is one likely to draw a crowd of onlookers. This is one of the penalties of the formal wedding which the informal one escapes.

—Vogue's Book of Brides

MUSIC

A WEDDING without music is as dull as it is unusual. At large and fashionable church weddings the ceremony is preceded by a program of instrumental music. During the service there may be choral singing or a solo, usually the popular "O Promise Me," sung by an opera or concert star, but at the ordinary church wedding it is in better taste to have the singing by the choir and its soloists, as a famous soloist suggests ostentation that does not seem appropriate to the occasion. The bride and her mother usually confer with the organist and choir leader, suggesting their favorite selections. If by any chance the family wishes to have an organist from another church, or a personal friend of the bride to play at a wedding, it is customary to secure permission from the regular organist, who in that case receives the customary fee exactly as if he had played. . . .

All musicians should be engaged well in advance. Organists and soloists have many engagements which cannot be broken, and good orchestras are in demand.

—The Bride's Book of Etiquette

ℰ ℰ ℰ

USUALLY at a wedding, even a large, formal church wedding, the organ alone supplies the music. But there may be also a full-vested choir to sing before the arrival of the wedding party, and to precede the bridal party to the altar, and to sing during the service. There may be a solo or a duet sung before the ceremony—"Lord Most Holy," or "The Voice That Breathed O'er Eden," or "Oh Perfect Love" by Barnby, "Oh Promise Me" by de Koven, "The SevenFold Amen," or "Thank God for Love" by Cezar Franck. A violin or harp are appropriate instruments at a wedding. Sometimes, especially at hotel weddings, "Faithful and True" is sung for the wedding march.

The "Lohengrin" wedding march is played for the processional, and the Mendelssohn wedding march as the recessional.

—Weddings: Modes, Manners and Customs

❦ ❦ ❦

SOLO singing between the betrothal and marriage parts of the service is not very frequent in smart weddings, although it is sometimes heard. In the weddings of the general public it must be usual, for whenever a certain type of girl has a friend with a voice she seems to want that friend to sing a solo at her wedding. It interrupts the service in a way one would think trying to the wedding group, who wait to walk from the chancel to the altar rail, while it is going on, and for that reason seems better omitted. But this is, of course, a matter of choice. Ours is against it.

—Vogue's Book of Brides

DUTIES OF THE MALE ATTENDANTS

THE BEST MAN

WHEN it is time, he and the groom drive to the church, and enter by the side door, usually into the vestry, or some other room at the front of the church. There they, with the clergyman, wait until they have the signal that the wedding party has arrived, and is ready to come down the aisle. Then, at the first notes of the wedding march, they follow the clergyman from this room, advance to the chancel-steps, and wait at the right of the steps. They turn and face the direction from which the bride is coming.

During the ceremony, the best man stands on the right of the groom, and a bit behind him. In the right time in the ceremony, he steps forward with the ring and hands it to the groom.

After the ceremony, the best man does not take part in the recessional, but instead goes to the vestry and hands to the clergyman the envelope containing the clergyman's fee. He sees too that arrangements have been made for the transportation of the clergyman to the reception. Then he collects the groom's hat and coat and takes them quickly to the door of the vestibule or to the groom in the waiting car.

—Weddings: Modes, Manners and Customs

THE USHERS

BESIDES attending rehearsals for a marriage, the ushers should each possess himself with a list of the relatives of the bride and groom with whom he is not acquainted, in order that they may be placed upon the proper side of the aisle and in due precedence according to kinship, the closest relatives being in front and others according to their remoteness. These lists are made familiar to the mind before the wedding day.

At the proper hour, they all call at the bride's residence for last orders, and she fastens a wedding favor of white blossoms and ribbons upon the left lapels of their coats. They go to the church a half hour before the ceremony is to be performed, and see that all things are in place, such as the kneeling rug, the ribbon across the aisle, etc., and that nothing is forgotten.

If guests arrive who are unknown to an usher, their names are asked, and by reference to memory or to a list, they are conducted to their proper places.

—Weddings Formal and Informal

AT the rehearsal, the groom may, if he wishes, assign places to the various ushers, assigning the ushers who know the members of the family and friends of the families to the center aisle. A "head usher" may be honored by being invited to escort the groom's mother and the bride's mother up the aisle, and he or another usher may be asked to see that the ushers arrive at the church promptly on the day of the wedding. Still another usher should be detailed to watch for the coming of the bride's mother and to notify the groom and the clergyman.

On the day of the wedding it is most important that the ushers arrive at the church at least an hour before the hour set for the ceremony, since wedding guests are early arrivals. The sexton indicates to them a convenient room for them to leave their hats and coats, and they will put on the boutonnières which the groom has sent to the church for them.

—Weddings: Modes, Manners and Customs

THE SECURITY DETAIL

A wedding, especially a large one, among the wealthy or the well known might attract uninvited guests, prompting the inclusion of the following advice in a popular book of etiquette:

As at balls, there is usually police protection at the church and at the house. A plain-clothes man is often assigned by the police department because pickpockets, male and female, slip into crowds. There should be a manservant at the curb to open the doors of cars, carriages, and taxis, and another servant is posted at the entrance to the house to stop intrusive strangers. At a large church wedding, the sexton or one of his assistants is stationed at the entrance of the gallery. If this part of the church has been reserved for servants, as is a common custom, he demands cards of admittance. If, on the other

hand, the gallery is open to the public, he uses his discretion in admitting people who have no invitations, turning away children or any one who might make a disturbance.

—Bride's Book of Etiquette

DUTIES OF THE MAID OR MATRON OF HONOR

AT the wedding itself, the details that are her chief concern are the bride's train and the bride's bouquet. Before the processional, she adjusts the bride's train, and after the ceremony, when the bride turns for the recessional, she must again arrange the bride's train. If the bride wears a short veil over her face, as some brides do, the maid of honor throws this back before she hands the bride her bouquet at the conclusion of the ceremony. Just before the ring is put on, the maid of honor hands her own bouquet to the bridesmaid next to her, and takes the bride's bouquet and holds it during this part of the ceremony.

At the end of the ceremony, the maid of honor hands the bride's bouquet to the bride, adjusts the bride's train, takes her own bouquet from the bridesmaid, and follows the bride and groom down the aisle. She allows a double number of spaces—eight—before she follows the bride and groom, and she walks down the aisle alone.

She goes with the other bridal attendants to the home of the bride, and there takes her place at the right of the bride, in the receiving line. . . .

If the bride has both a maid of honor and a matron of honor, there is a question as to the order in which they should walk. Sometimes they walk together, before the bride in the processional and after the bride and groom in the recessional. But usually each walks alone, the one closer to the bride in relationship or friendship being given the place of honor, in front of the bride. If the bride has two maids of honor and a matron of honor, usually

she plans to have the two maids of honor walk together in front of the matron of honor.

— Weddings: Modes, Manners and Customs

GUESTS AND SEATING

THE IDEAL GUEST

FAR too many people think that for a wedding guest there is no particular obligation other than to see, to hear—and often to eat!—as much as possible. As a return for all the hospitality, the impressive beauty, the courtesy, the friendliness that is extended to them, they often offer only a detached curiosity, an objective interest, a more or less detached participation. They are absorbed in their own reactions, often to the point of being most unpleasantly critical.

The kind-minded and therefore kind-mannered guest, on the other hand, realizes a personal responsibility to contribute graciousness and understanding, a friendly participation and appreciation of the infinite pains that have been expended to make a perfect wedding.

Perhaps a few suggestions to the wedding guest may be permitted:

First, answer the invitation promptly. Then send your wedding present three weeks or at least two weeks before the wedding, so that the bride will be able to write you a note of thinks before the last busy days before the wedding.

Even if you have received the magic card which will entitle you to a seat "within the ribbons" it is considerate to get to the church reasonably early. By so doing, you help the difficult task of the ushers.

The ideal guest will bow to the usher who meets her and will talk graciously and naturally to him as he escorts

her up the aisle. And she will, of course, accept without question the seat he assigns her.

At a wedding, whether at home or in church, the guests rise the very first moment that they hear the wedding march, and they remain standing during the entire ceremony.

When you are a guest at a church wedding, do not leave your place after the ceremony and recessional, until the bride's family, the groom's family, and the guests who are seated in the reserved seats ("within the ribbons") have been escorted down the aisle by the ushers. It is very important that the bride's mother should reach the house or ball-room, where she is to receive, as soon after the bride as possible, since she must be first to greet the wedding guests. Therefore it is not good form for the wedding guests to hurry to the reception on the heels of the family. They should proceed to their cars without haste, thus giving the wedding party time to get to their proper places in the receiving-line.

— Weddings: Modes, Manners and Customs

PROTOCOL FOR SEATING

AT church, those who are closest of kin to the bride and groom are placed nearest the altar, and gradations of relationship are recognized by the order of their seating, near or far from the wedding party.

— Weddings Formal and Informal

❦ ❦ ❦

USHERS will remember that the left side of the church is the "bride's side" and the right side is the "groom's side," and will, when they are escorting guests to seats, ask on which side the guest wishes to sit.

Also, if the wedding is a large one, several front pews on both sides will be marked off with white ribbons, and seats for these pews will be especially assigned either by means of a typewritten list given to the usher, or by special pew cards or inscribed visiting-cards.

An usher offers his arm to each lady as she arrives, asking her if she wishes to sit on the bride's side or the groom's side, and, as they walk up the aisle, making some pleasant comment about the seat that he can give her, or about the "beautiful day"—or the "rainy day!"—or something of the kind. The conversation should be carried on in a natural, dignified manner and in a low voice; there should not be an excess of gayety, nor on the other hand, should there be solemnity. If several ladies arrive together and there are many guests to be seated, the usher may offer his arm to one of the ladies and ask the rest to follow.

When the head usher has seated the groom's mother and father, he returns to the vestibule and escorts the bride's mother to her seat. Then he returns to the vestibule and takes his place (with the other ushers) at the head of the processional. The ushers walk together, two by two, in both the processional and the recessional.

— Weddings: Modes, Manners and Customs

ℰ℈ ℰ℈ ℰ℈

AT a perfectly managed wedding, the bride arrives exactly one minute (to give a last comer time to find a place) after the hour. Two or three servants have been sent to wait in the vestibule to help the bride and bridesmaids off with their wraps and hold them until they are needed after the ceremony. The groom's mother and father also are waiting in the vestibule. As the carriage of the bride's mother drives up, an usher goes as quickly as he can to tell the groom, and any brothers or sisters of the bride or groom, who are not to take part in the wedding procession and have arrived in their mother's carriage,

are now taken by ushers to their places in the front pews. The moment the entire wedding party is at the church, the doors between the vestibule and the church are *closed*. No one is seated after this, except the parents of the young couple.

The groom's mother goes down the aisle on the arm of the head usher and takes her place in the first pew on the right; the groom's father follows alone, and takes his place beside her; the same usher returns to the vestibule and immediately escorts the bride's mother, he should then have time to return to the vestibule and take his place in the procession. The beginning of the wedding march should sound just as the usher returns to the head of the aisle. To repeat: *No other person should be seated after the mother of the bride.* Guests who arrive later must stand in the vestibule or go into the gallery.

—Etiquette

CEREMONY

THE PROCESSION

The procession described below follows the plan appropriate to a church that has a chancel approached by a few stairs, typical of but not exclusive to Episcopal churches of the time. In a church with no chancel, the procession followed a similar pattern, although the attendants arranged themselves to the right and left of the bride and groom rather than in rows behind them.

THE formation of the procession is regulated by the arrangement of the church.

In Protestant churches the movements of the bridal procession are governed by the arrangement of aisles, while the grouping of the bridal party depends on the plan of chancel or pulpit. If there is a center aisle, the bride and her attendants pass up this aisle to chancel or

pulpit. If there are pews in the center and aisles on the sides, then the procession approaches the chancel or pulpit by the right-hand aisle and leaves by the left.

In an Episcopal church there will be a chancel with choir stalls and altar. In some of the modern churches of other denominations the altar is replaced by a stained-glass window, or, in the Baptist church, by the baptistery. In either case the bridal party is grouped in the chancel.

When the church has a high pulpit instead of a chancel, just below and in front of the pulpit there is usually a low, shallow, semicircular platform, with or without a railing. If there are a table and several chairs on the low platform, these are removed to make room for palms and flowers. The minister stands against the palms, and, like the bridal party, is almost on a level with the congregation.

If the vestry room or study opens from the right or left of the chancel, as in an Episcopal church, the minister, the groom, and his best man will enter the chancel through this door. If, however, the study opens directly into the main body of the church, right or left, the three men will enter through this door, and, passing the front pews, take their positions in front of and under the pulpit. If the study opens directly into the high pulpit, this door must be used, and the clergyman will lead the way down the steps to the lower platform.

Now with the setting clearly defined, we will form the wedding procession. In the vestry room or study are the groom, his best man, and the clergyman. And right here let us settle a question which often troubles the groom and best man. "How do they dispose of their hats and sticks?" These articles are left in the vestry room. If either the groom or the best man has a valet, the latter takes charge of them; otherwise an arrangement is made with the sexton or one of his assistants to carry them to the vestibule, where he waits for the recessional. The best man wears his gloves throughout the service. The groom removes the right glove as his bride approaches the chancel, holding it in his left hand, or, if he is very nervous, he may remove his right glove before he leaves the vestry room, but his right hand must be ungloved when he extends it to his bride. Lack of rehearsal in these details often causes confusion during the ceremony.

In the vestibule the bride, her father, and all of her attendants are waiting. The ushers lead the procession and they should be paired according to height. If a very tall and a very short man or a stout and thin man are paired, the guests may be reminded instantly of a comic strip in the evening paper. It is well to have the shortest ushers lead the procession. The bridesmaids, arranged with the same attention to height, come next, two by two, then the maid or matron of honor alone. The flower girl and the ring bearer or the two flower girls come next, and finally the bride on the arm of [her] father. If there are pages, they come last, bearing the bride's train. The bride is on the father's right, her left hand through his right arm.

With the first note of the wedding march, the clergyman, followed by the groom and the best man, steps from the vestry and walks slowly but not in march time to the opening in the railing, down the chancel, to the top of the steps, where the groom, with his best man behind him, awaits the coming of the bride.

At the same instant, the bride and her attendants start toward the chancel. The vestibule doors are held or fastened back, and the first two ushers act as pacemakers, saying very softly in time to the music, like army sergeants, "Left, left." The next pair of ushers take their time from the first, and the entire procession falls into step, always starting with the left foot. Four counts should be allowed between each pair of ushers and bridesmaids. Four more counts, and the maid or matron of honor steps forward, and at the end of four more counts, the flower girls. The bride then counts eight, and with her father steps into view, the pages, if there are any, carrying the train of her gown.

No counting must be done after the attendants step into the nave or body of the church, only in the vestibule, as on the wedding day nervousness may cause some one to count aloud, to the amusement of guests. If the pace is too slow or too fast, the organist may be asked to change his tempo, but this is necessary only when the organist is inexperienced. An experienced musician knows the correct time and the bridal party must keep step with the organ. It is sometimes necessary for the organist to drill the attendants. This point is stressed because a bridal procession is impressive only when it is correctly spaced and moves with dignity and precision.

When the ushers reach the steps leading to the chancel, they separate, right and left, mount the steps and walk into the chancel, where they turn, backs toward the choir stalls, facing each other. The bridesmaids separate in the same way and stand in front of the ushers, facing each other. The groom, meantime, has stepped to the foot of the chancel steps to meet the bride, his best man on his right. When the maid or matron of honor reaches the chancel, she stops at the foot of the steps, or on one of the lower steps, according to their number, but a little to the left, and the best man takes his place on a line with her, but at the right.

When the bride arrives at the chancel steps, she takes her left hand from her father's arm, shifts her bouquet, or prayer book, from her right hand to her left, and gives her right hand to the groom, who slips it into his left arm to lead her up the steps.

If the service is to be read at the foot of the chancel, which seems to be the more popular custom, the groom takes her right hand in his left and they face the clergyman in this position.

The father stands directly behind the maid of honor or the bride, and the flower girls are stationed where they give the best effect, usually to the right and left, and beyond the best man and maid of honor.

The exact positions will be determined by the size of the chancel and the number of steps.

—*The Bride's Book of Etiquette*

IF the ceremony is divided, the first part read at the foot of the chancel and the second part at the chancel rail, the ushers and the bridesmaids remain in position, but the maid of honor and the best man follow the bride and the groom up the steps, between the double line of attendants, to the chancel rail, taking their positions.

Now for the various steps in the ceremony.

On reaching the chancel, and before the service begins, the bride hands her bouquet, or whatever she may carry in its stead, to her maid of honor, who holds it until the ceremony is over, returning it to the bride before the latter turns to face the congregation for the recessional. If the bride removes her left glove, she hands this also to her maid of honor. During this time an anthem may be sung by the choir or a soloist may sing softly. The best man has the wedding ring in his vest pocket so that he can produce it instantly the clergyman gives the signal. Immediately the father or male relative has given away the bride, he leaves the bridal party and joins his wife or family in the first left-hand pew.

— The Bride's Book of Etiquette

Different expertness on correctness advocated different approaches to the giving of the ring during the ceremony:

THE wedding ring is an important—and anxiety-compelling—care of the best man. At the appropriate time in the ceremony he hands it to the bridegroom. The groom does not hand it directly to the clergyman, but instead hands it to the bride who in turn gives it to the clergyman. In this way is symbolized the idea that the clergyman receives the ring from them both and that it is given the blessing of the Church. The clergyman completes the cycle of the progress of the ring by returning it to the

groom, who, when the clergyman indicates, by the words, "With this ring, I thee wed," puts it on the bride's finger.

Before this part of the ceremony, the bride has, if she wears gloves, removed her left glove. She may have removed it in the vestibule (although this is rarely done, since it means another item to be kept in mind—and in hand) or she may remove it and hand it to her maid of honor before the ceremony, or she may have slit the third finger of her glove.

—Weddings: Modes, Manners and Customs

ஃ ஃ ஃ

WHEN it is time for the ring, the best man produces it from his pocket. If in the handling from best man to groom, to clergyman, to groom again, and finally to the bride's finger, it should slip and fall, the best man must pick it up if he can without searching; if not, he quietly produces the duplicate which all careful best men carry in the other waistcoat pocket, and the ceremony proceeds. The lost ring—or the unused extra one—is returned to the jeweler's the next day. Which ring, under the circumstances, the bride keeps, is a question as hard to answer as that of the Lady or the Tiger. Would she prefer the substitute ring that was actually the one she was married with? Or the one her husband bought and had marked for her? Or would she prefer not to have a substitute ring and have the whole wedding party on their knees searching? She alone can decide. Fortunately, even if the clergyman is very old and his hand shaky, a substitute is seldom necessary.

The wedding ring must not be put above the engagement ring. On her wedding day a bride either leaves her engagement ring at home when she goes to church or wears it on her right hand.

—Etiquette

— 140 —

THE RECESSIONAL

WHEN the ceremony is over, the maid of honor hands the bride her bouquet, and, as the bride turns for the recessional, the maid of honor arranges her train and veil. The bride puts her left hand in the groom's right arm, and they lead the recessional.

The double space in the processional is used in the recessional also, eight beats being counted between the bride and groom and the maid of honor.

Following the bride and groom comes the maid of honor or the matron of honor, walking alone, as she did in the processional.

Following the maid of honor come the bridesmaids, walking together, two by two, as they did in the processional.

Last in the recessional come the ushers, also walking together, two by two, as they did in the processional.

The best man waits until the recessional is started and then goes to the vestry to attend to his duties. To the clergyman he hands the fee that the groom has given to him for this purpose. He makes sure that arrangements have been made for the transportation of the clergyman and his wife (if he has one) to the reception. And, if the sexton has not made arrangements to have the groom's hat and coat and stick taken to the groom at the entrance of the church, the best man does this.

If there are flower girls, they usually walk before the bride and groom.

— Weddings: Modes, Manners and Customs

AFTER THE RECESSIONAL

AFTER the recessional, the assembled guests take their seats or stand in their places, for they should not leave the church until the ushers have returned and have escorted down the aisle the members of the immediate families and

the intimate friends of the families who have occupied the reserved pews. As soon as the bride and her attendants have reached the vestibule of the church, the head usher hastens to the first left-hand pew to escort the bride's mother down the aisle, the next usher escorting the groom's mother, and the other ushers escorting the other members of the families and friends in the pews "within the ribbons" or otherwise reserved. This method makes it possible for the bride's mother and the groom's mother to reach their cars at the front of the church as quickly as possible and to arrive at the reception and take their places in the receiving line before the arrival of the guests.

—*Weddings: Modes, Manners and Customs*

CHAPTER 8

A House Wedding

Weddings that took place at home—usually the bride's parents', of course—could range almost as widely as church weddings in their degree of formality and elaborateness. Particularly for those with very deep pockets, and the inclination, a house wedding could become quite a production, but it did not need to be in order to be quite correct.

AT HOME IN HIGH SOCIETY

When one's home was far from humble, one could have a wedding at the decidedly more showy end of the spectrum, as illustrated by the two weddings described below.

BY the 1870s grand American weddings, held in the bride's home, were also very spectacular occasions indeed, and magnificent were the arrangements made for them. A low platform was usually constructed at one end of the drawing-room, for the bride, bridegroom and priest to stand upon. Swathes of flowers and greenery turned the area into a sylvan bower, with a vast bridal bell, made of fresh white blooms, hanging in the centre above the principals' heads. Garlands of flowers and greenery festooned

the house, often criss-crossing the rooms like Christmas decorations; the chandeliers dripped with foliage; floral monograms of the bride's and bridegroom's initials decorated the walls; potted palms concealed the fireplace, and horseshoes made of flowers filled in the gaps. In May 1874, all these preparations were made at the White House for the President's daughter, Nellie Grant, the pet of the nation, who was about to marry an Englishman and sail off across the Atlantic, much to the disgust of her parents and the country as a whole. The bridegroom was Algernon Sartoris, nephew of the actress Fanny Kemble; a young man with fine moustaches, melodious singing voice, and a tendency to drink.

—And the Bride Wore . . .

ᏃᎦ ᏃᎦ ᏃᎦ

A House Wedding:
De Pedroso and Berghmans

AT the wedding of Camilla Berghmans and Don Jose de Pedrosa, secretary of the Spanish legation, last week, at Glengary, the country seat of the bride's mother, Mrs. McAllister Laughton, the bridal party came up from Philadelphia in a steamboat, and were conveyed to the shore in a rowboat, whose sides and gunwales were completely hidden by flowers, and whose oars were covered with roses, while the rowers were in costume. A wide hallway runs through the house, and the door at the back opens on to a stretch of green lawn that slopes down to the Delaware. A strip of crimson carpet was spread from this doorway over the green lawn to the landing-place on the river, and over this the bridal party walked, the bridesmaids in white embroidered crêpe lisse over satin, tulle veils and light opera wraps of pale pink, carrying bouquets of apple blossoms. A little room at the end of a long suite had been fitted up as a chapel. The altar was

draped with ivory satin and old lace, and there Archbishop Ryan, in purple vestments, celebrated the nuptial-mass. After the breakfast and reception, as the bride came down the stairway in her travelling costume of dark blue, she paused half way and flung her wedding bouquet into the group of bridesmaids assembled at the foot of the stairs. These eagerly sprung for it, and unless the sign fails, the fair maid who caught it will be the next bride of the group. A double row of guests assembled on the lawn and showered the bride and groom with rice and white slippers.

— Wedding Etiquette and Usages of Polite Society

HOME OR CHURCH?

For most of polite society, a house wedding was similar to that in a church, in most particulars, but with some modifications. The degree of formality, in either place, was set by the bride's choice of attire. If she wore a traditional white wedding dress, the wedding was formal, and all other details of the ceremony ought to conform to that standard. A clergyman would most likely be the one to perform the marriage rites in a home, as in a church. There would not likely be an organist or a full choir at home, but having a soloist would be feasible, and the wedding marches from "Lohengrin" and by Mendelssohn, *de rigueur* at home as in church, could be played by a pianist or, at a large home wedding, a small orchestra, which might be hired for the reception as well. Other key similarities and differences are detailed in the following comparison:

The House Wedding

A HOUSE wedding involves slightly less expenditure but has the disadvantage of limiting the number of guests. The ceremony is exactly the same as that in a church, excepting that the procession advances through an aisle of white satin ribbons from the stairs down which the bridal

party descends, to the improvised altar. A small space near the altar is fenced off with other ribbons, for the family. There is a low rail of some sort back of which the clergyman stands, and something for the bride and groom to kneel on during the prayers of the ceremony. The prayer bench is usually about six or eight inches high, and between three and four feet long; at the back of it an upright on either end supports a crosspiece—or altar rail. It can be made in roughest fashion by any carpenter, or amateur, as it is entirely hidden under leaves and flowers. On the kneeling surface of the bench are placed cushions rather than flowers, because the latter stain. All caterers have the necessary standards to which ribbons are tied, like the wires to telegraph poles. The top of each standard is usually decorated with a spray of white flowers.

At a house wedding the bride's mother stands at the door of the drawing-room—or wherever the ceremony is to be—and receives people as they arrive. But the groom's mother merely takes her place near the altar with the rest of the immediate family. The ushers are purely ornamental, unless the house is so large that "pews" have been installed, and the guests are seated as in a church. Otherwise the guests stand wherever they can find places behind the aisle ribbons. Just before the bride's entrance, her mother goes forward and stands in the reserved part of the room. The ushers go up to the top of the stairway. The wedding march begins and the ushers come down two and two, followed by the bridesmaids, exactly as in a church, the bride coming last on her father's arm. The clergyman and the groom and best man have, if possible, reached the altar by another door. If the room has only one door, they go up the aisle a few moments before the bridal procession starts.

The chief difference between a church and house wedding is that the bride and groom do not take a single step together. The groom meets her at the point where the service is read. After the ceremony, there is no recessional. The clergyman withdraws, an usher removes the

prayer bench, and the bride and groom merely turn where they stand, and receive the congratulations of their guests, unless, of course, the house is so big that they receive in another room.

When there is no recessional, the groom always kisses the bride before they turn to receive their guests—it is against all tradition for any one to kiss her before her husband does.

There are seldom many bridal attendants at a house wedding, two to four ushers, and one to four bridesmaids, unless the house is an immense one.

In the country a house wedding includes one in a garden, with a wedding procession under the trees, and tables out on the lawn—a perfect plan for California or other rainless States, but difficult to arrange on the Atlantic seaboard where rain is too likely to spoil everything.

—Etiquette

For a house wedding in the best taste, brides could heed the following advice:

WHEN the bride decides to have her wedding in her home, the same general plans are followed as in a church wedding. For the bride who does not wish the elaborate pageantry of a large church wedding, a house wedding represents the charming intimacy of being married in a simple artistic manner, in her own home, in the midst of her family and the close friends whom she chooses to have with her on her wedding-day.

A house wedding is not so expensive, of course, as a church wedding. And even with a limited space and with a limited budget, a house wedding can be planned so that it will be a memory-making event of jewel-like perfection. To do this takes taste and cleverness in capitalizing every element. Too often we see people of a simple background, people who when they give an ordinary

party have impeccable taste, who when the word "wedding" is mentioned, are a bit overwhelmed. Instead of glorifying simplicity, they decide to disregard simplicity as if they were a bit afraid of it, and strain for some insincere effect that can be classified more as "splurge" than as taste. This is, of course, a mistake.

—Weddings: Modes, Manners and Customs

DECORATIONS

A home was to look just as beautiful as would a church, and it was appropriate to decorate with a great deal of care and attention, whether one's wedding was large, small, formal, or informal.

A LARGE wedding in a home or hotel ballroom requires carefully planned decorations. First, the effect of an altar must be given at the end of a large room in which the ceremony is to be performed. For the background there may be a screen of smilax, asparagus fern, laurel, or wood ferns, according to the season. On either side should be high vases filled with flowers. An altar can be rented or it can be built of ordinary lumber, or even an empty packing box, covered with satin or lace, brocade, or a piece of embroidery. In front of this altar is placed a long narrow stool or prayer bench, or a pillow, appropriately covered to harmonize with the altar, on which the bridal couple will kneel. On the improvised altar are a rack for the prayer book and simple vases filled with white flowers. High candlesticks on either side of the altar, or against the screen, are effective. Such an altar lends such dignity to the occasion that it is frequently used in homes of families who are neither Catholics nor Episcopalians.

The next step in decorating is an aisle for the bridal party. White ribbons held in place by tall, white standards

are used for this purpose. The standards may be rented from florists or caterers. The aisle must be broad enough for the bridal party to walk two abreast without being crowded. Sometimes the ribbons are held in place by ushers whose duties are otherwise nominal at a house wedding, or by children dressed alike and drilled in the service.

Flowers for the house wedding, exclusive of the altar or screen, may be as colorful as the bride likes them. Pink roses with blue larkspur, yellow jonquils with white narcissus, forsythia and dog-wood, climbing roses and marguerites, cornflowers and apple blossoms, are lovely for spring and summer, while for September weddings nothing is handsomer than the brilliant-toned dahlias. For October and November autumn leaves and chrysanthemums are preferred, and for winter roses. Quite generally the decorations of the table for the bridal party are in white and green, but if the bride has a fondness for any particular flower or color, this is used in the dining room and throughout the house.

When means permit, much trouble may be saved by making a contract with a florist, who will supply everything from the altar decorations to the boutonnières for the ushers. [An] awning furnishes protection against the elements and keeps back the curious who otherwise might crowd too closely. [A] carpet protects both delicately shod feet and the rugs of the hostess. Therefore both are essential for a church wedding or for a large house wedding. When the church ceremony is followed by a reception at the house, there must be an awning at both places. Summing it up, awnings may be dispensed with only at a country or suburban wedding in fair weather, or at a town wedding in church or home when the ceremony is performed in the presence of relatives and a few intimate friends and when the bride wears her going-away gown. . . .

For a house wedding the awning and carpet are sometimes supplied by the caterer, or the bride's mother may order them directly from firms that make a specialty of renting them. When the wedding is held in a hotel or assembly hall, the management supplies the awning and the carpet.

— The Bride's Book of Etiquette

ᔆᗋ ᔆᗋ ᔆᗋ

FOR the simple home wedding, the decorations will, consistently, be simple. Flowers in vases and bowls—wild flowers, or garden flowers, or hothouse flowers—are placed in convenient places, blooming plants are used, or only greenery of various kinds. For the spring and summer wedding branches of flowering trees and rambler roses may be used. Mountain laurel is often used. In summer too bowls of wild flowers and meadow grasses are lovely, and so are old-fashioned garden flowers—hollyhocks, snapdragons, larkspur, sweetpeas, daffodils, and so forth. For the autumn wedding we have the gorgeous colorings of the autumn leaves, goldenrod, chrysanthemums, cosmos, hydrangeas, asters.

The most effective place for the ceremony is usually before a mantel or a fireplace, or in a bow window, or between two windows in the living-room or drawing-room. This space can be banked with greens, branches of white pine and hemlock, ropes of mountain pine, winter berries, or, in the summer, with wild flowers, or, at any season, with large forms of greenery of some kind covered with smilax.

Garlands of smilax or foliage or flowers are sometimes used most effectively for the background of the place where the ceremony is to be performed. Or we may, if we are fortunate enough to own one, use a lovely tapestry or a beautiful piece of old silk. Or we may use a lovely old

chest flanked by tall stately Italian or Spanish candle-sticks or candelabra.

At the ends of this improvised background, to gain harmony in the unit of decoration, there should be two tall items of decoration. Tall floor candlesticks containing cathedral candles are especially appropriate and hand-some for outlining this sacred ceremony-place, and so are the simple tall stands for the always-graceful trailing ivy. Very tall, simple white vases of flowers are beautiful, especially when a few white calla lilies are used in tall, white crystal or glass vases. If a prayer bench is placed in front of the improvised altar, it is covered with flowers or leaves or greenery on the ends, but in the center, where the couple are to kneel, cushions are placed, usually of white satin.

The rest of the room should be left as much as possible as it ordinarily is. Heavy central pieces of furniture are, of course, moved to the sides of the room, and it is well to leave several chairs in position so that any older guests may sit, if they wish.

The problem of music for the house wedding is not easy, but appropriateness should be the plan. No music is better than poor music. The wedding march may be played by a small stringed orchestra of a few pieces, or by a violin or a harp or a piano alone, or it may be sung.

— Weddings: Modes, Manners and Customs

ATTENDANTS

THE number of attendants in a house wedding usually depends on the size of the home, for "home," in these days, is often an apartment of a size that does not accom-modate a large wedding party, the limited space forbid-ding much of a "processional." Sometimes the bride has

no attendant, but usually she has a maid of honor or a matron of honor. Or she may have this chief attendant and a flower girl. If she wishes and if the size and arrangement of the room warrant a larger party, she may also have two bridesmaids or even four. Usually there are no ushers, since there are no duties for them, although it is correct to have ushers if the couple wish. The groom has a best man.

As the guests arrive, the bride's mother, the hostess of the occasion, stands at the door of the room in which the ceremony is to be performed, and receives the guests. Often the bride's father greets the guests with her. The bride and her attendant and the groom and his attendant do not appear before they enter for the ceremony. This is true even in an informal wedding.

When the wedding party is ready, the bride's mother is notified and she takes her place in the part of the room reserved for the family of the bride, on the left of the room. On the right of the ceremony-place stand the mother and father of the groom and the members of their immediate family.

At the first notes of the wedding march or at some other signal, the clergyman enters the room and takes his place at the improvised altar, facing the assembled guests. Then the groom enters with his best man, and they take their places at the right of the altar. If there are ushers, they lead the procession, two by two. If there are no ushers but are to be, say, two bridesmaids, they come first, together. Then comes the maid of honor, alone, followed by a flower girl, if there is one. Or the flower girl may be first in the processional. Last come the bride and her father.

The maid of honor stands at the bride's left, to help her with her train and flowers and glove, and the best man stands at the right of the groom to produce the ring at the appropriate time.

—Weddings: Modes, Manners and Customs

AT HOME

Not every bride and groom had the White House or a steamboat at their disposal. That needn't have dampened their spirits, nor meant that they could not conform to what etiquette required. Here is a peek at an "ordinary" at-home wedding day of the 1920s.

IF the wedding is to be at noon, dawn will not have much more than broken before the house—at least below stairs—becomes bustling.

Even if the wedding is to be at four o'clock, it will still be early in the morning when the business of the day begins. But let us suppose it is to be at noon; if the family is one that is used to assembling at an early breakfast table, it is probable that the bride herself will come down for this last meal alone with her family. They will, however, not be allowed to linger long at the table. The caterer will already be clamoring for possession of the dining-room—the florist will by that time already have dumped heaps of wire and greens into the middle of the drawing-room, if not beside the table where the family are still communing with their eggs. The door-bell has long ago begun to ring. At first there are telegrams and special delivery letters, then as soon as the shops open, come the last-moment wedding presents, notes, messages and the insistent clamor of the telephone.

Next, excited voices in the hall announce members of the family who come from a distance. They all want to kiss the bride, they all want rooms to dress in, they all want to talk. Also comes the hairdresser to do the bride's or her mother's or aunt's or grandmother's hair, or all of them; the manicure, the masseuse—anyone else that may have been thought necessary to give final beautifying touches to any or all of the female members of the household. The dozen and one articles from the caterer are meantime being carried in at the basement door; made dishes, and dishes in the making, raw materials of which others are to be made; folding chairs, small tables,

chinaware, glassware, napery, knives, forks and spoons —
it is a struggle to get in or out of the kitchen or area door.

The bride's mother consults the florist for the third and
last time as to whether the bridal couple had not better
receive in the library because of the bay window which
lends itself easily to the decoration of a background, and
because the room, is, if anything, larger than the drawing-
room. And for the third time, the florist agrees about the
advantage of the window but points out that the library
has only one narrow door and that the drawing-room is
much better, because it has two wide ones and guests
going into the room will not be blocked in the doorway by
others coming out.

The best man turns up and wants the bride's luggage.

The head usher comes to ask whether the Joneses to
be seated in the fourth pew are the tall dark ones or the
blond ones, and whether he had not better put some of
the Titheringtons who belong in the eighth pew also in
the seventh, as there are nine Titheringtons and the Emi-
nents in the seventh pew are only four.

A bridesmaid-elect hurries up the steps, runs into the
best man carrying out the luggage; much conversation
and giggling and guessing as to where the luggage is
going. Best man very important, also very noble and
silent. Bridesmaid shrugs her shoulders, dashes up to the
bride's room and dashes down again.

More presents arrive. The furniture movers have come
and are carting lumps of heaviness up the stairs to the
attic and down the stairs to the cellar. It is all very like an
anthill. Some are steadily going forward with the business
in hand, but others who have become quite bewildered,
seem to be scurrying aimlessly this way and that, picking
something up only to put it down again.

The Drawing-Room

Here, where the bride and groom are to receive, one
can not tell yet what the decoration is to be. Perhaps it is

a hedged-in garden scene, a palm grove, a flowering recess, a screen and canopy of wedding bells—but a bower of foliage of some sort is gradually taking shape.

The Dining-Room

The dining-room, too, blossoms with plants and flowers. Perhaps its space and that of a tent adjoining is filled with little tables, or perhaps a single row of camp chairs stands flat against the walls, and in the center of the room, the dining table pulled out to its farthest extent, is being decked with trimmings and utensils which will be needed later when the spaces left at intervals for various dishes shall be occupied. Preparation of these dishes is meanwhile going on in the kitchen.

The Kitchen

The caterer's chefs in white cook's caps and aprons are in possession of the situation, and their assistants run here and there, bringing ingredients as they are told; or perhaps the caterer brings everything already prepared, in which case the waiters are busy unpacking the big tin boxes and placing the *bain-marie* (a sort of fireless cooker receptacle in a tank of hot water) from which the hot food is to be served. Huge tubs of cracked ice in which the ice cream containers are buried are already standing in the shade of the areaway or in the back yard.

Last Preparations

Back again in the drawing-room, the florist and his assistants are still trying and tacking and arranging and adjusting branches and garlands and sheaves and bunches, and the floor is a litter of twigs and strings and broken branches. The photographer is asking that the central decoration be finished so he can group his pictures, the florist assures him that he is as busy as possible.

The house is as cold as open windows can make it, to keep the flowers fresh, and to avoid stuffiness. The doorbell continues its ringing, and the parlor maid finds herself a contestant in a marathon, until someone decides that card envelopes and telegrams had better be left in the front hall.

A first bridesmaid arrives. She at least is on time. All decoration activity stops while she is looked at and admired. Panic seizes someone! The time is too short, nothing will be ready! Someone else says the bridesmaid is far too early, there is no end of time.

Upstairs everyone is still dressing. The father of the bride (one would suppose him to be the bridegroom at least) is trying on most of his shirts, the floor strewn with discarded collars! The mother of the bride is hurrying into her wedding array as well as to superintend the finishing touches to her daughter's dress and veil.

—Etiquette

CHAPTER 9

The Reception

It was entirely appropriate for the wedding reception to be held at the bride's home, and many were, and equally to rent a ballroom or other private space in a hotel or country club. Church rooms or rectory parlors were also sometimes used. Careful attention was given to the decoration of the reception facility, as it had been to the site of the ceremony itself. The bride and groom and their families and attendants all had duties to perform at the reception, and the guests had their part to play correctly as well. Once the greetings and congratulations were completed in the receiving line, the highlight of the reception was its food, and especially the cake or cakes.

THE RECEIVING LINE

ARRANGEMENT OF THE BRIDAL PARTY

IN planning the wedding reception, there is always the discussion as to who is to be in the receiving line. Although we are supposed to be convinced that the "receiving line" is a thing of the past, as a matter of fact when we go to weddings we see—the receiving line, and usually quite a flourishing receiving line. And it is easy to

understand why. Weddings are reunion-izers, and it is natural that the people most concerned with the wedding take their places to receive their friends.

The mother of the bride, who is the hostess of the wedding, stands at or near the entrance of the room in which her guests are to enter. She is the first to greet the guests. If the father of the bride is an "amply cordial" man, he will probably wish to stand beside his wife, to greet their friends. If he prefers to greet the guests after they have passed down the receiving line, he may do that, having a wider scope for the dispensing of his hospitality. Or he may stand for a while in the receiving line, and then "mingle with the guests."

The bride's mother invites the mother and father of the groom to stand in the receiving line to greet the friends of their family and to greet, or to meet, the friends of the bride's family. This too seems a natural and simple way of arranging these hospitable meetings. The groom's mother may stand next to the bride's mother, and therefore at her son's left, or the groom's father may stand next to the bride's mother, and his wife next to him, still next to her son. Or the groom's mother may stand on or near the end of the receiving line, next to the last bridesmaid, but this often gives an unpleasant impression of thoughtless placing, even though the groom's mother may have chosen this place. The groom's father may, like the bride's father, prefer to "circulate," greeting groups of friends beyond the fixed compass of the receiving line.

The bride and groom stand in the line beyond the bride's mother, the bride standing on the right of her husband.

Next to the bride, on her right, stands her chief attendant, the maid of honor or matron of honor, and beyond her, the bridesmaids.

—Weddings: Modes, Manners and Customs

CONDUCT OF THE GUESTS

WHAT you should say in congratulating a bridal couple depends on how well you know one, or both of them. But remember it is a breach of good manners to congratulate a bride on having secured a husband.

If you are unknown to both of them, and in a long queue, it is not even necessary to give your name. You merely shake hands with the groom, say a formal word or two such as "Congratulations!"; shake hands with the bride, say "I wish you every happiness!" and pass on.

If you know them fairly well, you may say to him "I hope your good luck will stay with you always!" or "I certainly do congratulate you!" and to her "I hope your whole life will be one long happiness," or if you are much older than she, "You look too lovely, dear Mary, and I hope you will always be as radiant as you look to-day!" Or, if you are a woman and a relative or really close friend, you kiss the groom, saying, "All the luck in the world to you, dear Jim, she certainly is lovely!" Or, kissing the bride, "Mary, darling, every good wish in the world to you!"

To all the above, the groom and bride answer merely "Thank you."

A man might say to the groom "Good luck to you, Jim, old man!" Or, "She is the most lovely thing I have ever seen!" And to her, "I hope you will have every happiness!" Or, "I was just telling Jim how lucky I think he is! I hope you will both be very happy!" Or, if a very close friend, also kissing the bride, "All the happiness you can think of isn't as much as I wish you, Mary dear!" But it cannot be too much emphasized that promiscuous kissing among the guests is an offense against good taste.

To a relative, or old friend of the bride, but possibly a stranger to the groom, the bride always introduces her husband saying, "Jim, this is Aunt Kate!" Or, Mrs. Neighbor,

you know Jim, don't you?" Or formally, "Mrs. Faraway, may I present my husband?"

The groom on the approach of an old friend of his, says, "Mary, this is cousin Carrie." Or, "Mrs. Denver, do you know Mary?" Or, "Hello, Steve, let me introduce you to my wife; Mary, this is Steve Michigan." Steve says "How do you do, Mrs. Smartlington!" And Mary says, "Of course, I have often heard Jim speak of you!"

The bride with a good memory thanks each arriving person for the gift sent her: "Thank you so much for the lovely candlesticks," or "I can't tell you how much I love the dishes!" The person who is thanked says, "I am so glad you like it (or them)," or "I am so glad! I hoped you might find it useful." Or, "I didn't have it marked, so that in case you have a duplicate, you can change it."

Conversation is never a fixed grouping of words that are learned or recited like a part in a play; the above examples are given more to indicate the sort of things people in good society usually say. There is, however, one rule: Do not launch into long conversation or details of *yourself*, how you feel or look or what happened to you, or what *you* wore when you were married! Your subject matter must not deviate from the young couple themselves, their wedding, their future.

Also be brief in order not to keep those behind waiting longer than necessary. If you have anything particular to tell them, you can return later when there is no longer a line. But even then, long conversation, especially concerning yourself, is out of place.

—Etiquette

A guest who left after passing down the receiving line would not have breached any rules of etiquette. Of course, however, most stayed for the festivities to come, which often included music and dancing.

DUTIES OF THE BEST MAN AND USHERS

THE BEST MAN

DURING the reception the best man stands within beckoning distance of the groom, so that he may be signaled to attend to any service that the groom wishes. During the wedding breakfast, he may briefly substitute for his executive and professional duties the social one of being the honored guest to sit on the right of the bride, and when the dancing begins he is again honored by being awarded the second dance with the bride—her first being, of course, with the groom. But soon his dancing may be interrupted by the call of "duty," and he goes with the groom to the room set apart for them, and helps the groom to dress and pack for the wedding journey. If he is the methodical person that he should be, he has brought the groom's luggage to the bride's house before the wedding, and he has purchased the tickets for the journey.

—Weddings: Modes, Manners and Customs

USHERS

The ushers show guests to the receiving line and thence to the refreshments. In particular:

IF the bride has requested it, the usher who presents guests to her, conducts them to her father and mother, and then to the groom's parents, and introduces them by name. Each woman thus conducted takes the usher's arm, and if she is accompanied by a man, he walks by her side, or follows and is presented at the same time.

When all the guests, or nearly all of them, have been introduced, a part of the ushers may escort guests to the refreshment room, provided there is not a formal

breakfast, in which case the hostess has arranged for the serving of this feast.

Ushers see that no one is neglected, thus aiding the bridesmaids in a mutual kindness and hospitality.

After most of the guests have departed and the bride and groom have gone, ushers are at liberty to take leave of their hosts, their duties having been completed, unless the hostess requires further services, which of course they perform gladly.

It is etiquette that a call be made upon the bride's mother within a week, if distance allows, but if calling is impossible, a note of thanks and kindly inquiry is *de rigueur*. Any other thoughtful recognition of a parent's loneliness after a daughter has left home, is a mark of tender consideration, and fine feeling.

— Weddings Formal and Informal

THE WEDDING FEAST

It was not in fact a requirement that a *feast*, per se, be served. As long as cake was not overlooked, a simple tea could be perfectly appropriate. Many people did serve a full meal, however — often a wedding breakfast, served, despite its name, at noon after a morning wedding, and consisting of a luncheon menu.

SERVING

THE wedding food may be served as either a "sit-down" meal or a "stand-up" meal. If there are very few guests, they are usually seated at one large table; and there may or may not be a separate bridal table. If there are many guests, there is usually the bride's table, a second table called the "parents' table" at which are the fathers and mothers, the clergyman and his wife, the nearest relatives, and the most distinguished guests, the

other guests being seated, according to place cards or their own inclinations, at tables seating four or six.

The "stand-up" meal, the buffet, is always correct and is much easier and simpler than the "sit-down" meal. The buffet meal means that the food will be arranged—and the buffet table can be most artistically and conveniently arranged—on one long table. A buffet is especially appropriate for serving the kind of food—the "glorified tea"—served after an afternoon wedding. As in all buffet meals, the guests, having claimed plates, napkins, and silver from the friendly piles on the table, serve themselves to the food.

With the buffet meal too, there is usually a bride's table, but naturally any other set table is omitted.

—Weddings: Modes, Manners and Customs

SEATING THE GUESTS

TO seat the guests at a wedding feast, with exactly the correct acknowledgment of the significance of each one, requires the famous "wisdom of the serpent and harmlessness of the dove." It is the prayer of the hostess of every wedding that she will emerge from the wedding festivities without "hurting the feelings" of any relative or friend. But there is something about a wedding that calls forth all the dear little egotisms which are usually ashamed of themselves, and which therefore remain hidden in the depths of one's being. One of the blessings of the clearly-defined traditions of etiquette is that they suggest ways of correctly seating wedding guests.

The bride and her mother, if they are wise, will make a diagram of the table and will arrange (and rearrange!) the seating, so that it will achieve the ultimate of tactful placing. Place-cards are, of course, a great convenience.

The larger the wedding reception, the less difficult the seating of the guests, paradoxical as that may sound. For

when there are many people invited, the bride and groom, maid of honor and best man, bridesmaids and ushers, are usually seated at a "bride's table," placed either in the center of the room, where all may see and admire, or else in a separate room, but still visible to the guests. At a large house reception the rest of the guests are usually not seated, but are served from one large buffet table, beautifully decorated and bountifully laden with good and artistically arranged things.

—Weddings: Modes, Manners and Customs

THE BRIDE'S TABLE

AT the wedding feast the bride's table is to the dining-room what the bride is to the wedding processional. The decorations on the table may be simple or elaborate, and are usually all-white.

At the bride's table, the bride and groom sit at the "head" of the table, side by side, the bride at the right of the groom. The best man sits at the right of the bride, and the maid or matron of honor at the left of the groom. The bridesmaids and ushers are seated alternately, and according to the bride's knowledge of their congeniality. If some of the attendants are married and their wives or husbands, as the case may be, are not of the wedding party, it is customary for the bride and groom to invite them to join the wedding party at the bridal table. For convenience, place cards are usually used for the assignment of places at the bridal table.

Sometimes, at a large reception, when there is a bridal table but only a maid of honor and a best man in the wedding party, the young friends of the bride and groom are seated at the bride's table, and placed as they would be at any formal luncheon or dinner.

—Weddings: Modes, Manners and Customs

THE PARENTS' TABLE

NEXT in importance to the bride's table is the table at which sit the parents of the bridal couple. Here, too, there are certain definite traditions as to seating-arrangements. The bride's mother is the "head" of the table, since she is the hostess. At her right is the groom's father, the man guest of honor. Opposite the bride's mother is the bride's father, and on his right is the groom's mother, the woman guest of honor. On the left of the bride's mother is the minister, and on the bride's father's left is the minister's wife, if he has one, and if not, an important relative of the bride's or groom's family.

At this table, too, will be seated close relatives of both families, distinguished guests, and close friends of the family. Any sisters or brothers of the bride and groom who are not in the wedding party will also be invited to sit at this table.

— Weddings: Modes, Manners and Customs

TOASTS

Toasts were made . . .

AS a rule at the end of the meal at the bride's table. The best man usually—but anybody may—proposes the health of the bride and groom. (They, of course, may not drink to themselves.) The groom returns thanks for the bride. No set speeches are worth giving. Only words that come spontaneously can possibly suit the occasion, and a very few words are sufficient.

— Vogue's Book of Brides

THE most festive and gala part of the wedding-day is the wedding feast, for whether it is the most simple of teas or the most sumptuous of dinners, there is about it an air of happy festivity.

A printed menu may be placed on each table at a wedding breakfast. At the top may be tied a tiny white bow, and the intertwined initials of the surnames of the bride and groom may be embossed in silver. At the bottom of the card is printed the date, and, if the wedding breakfast is held in a hotel, the name of the hotel is often printed in the other corner on the bottom of the card.

Combination Menu for the Wedding Feast

SUGGESTIONS of dishes appropriate for a wedding breakfast, a reception, or a supper:

FIRST COURSE:
Choice of these:

Hot:
Bouillon or consommé: chicken, tomato, mushroom, clear green turtle.
Purée: tomato, mushroom, chestnut, chicken with rice
Clam broth or oyster broth
Canapé: mushroom

Cold:
Jellied bouillon or jellied consommé: chicken, tomato, essence of tomato, chicken gumbo
Clam juice cocktail
Shrimp, crab flake, or lobster cocktail
Fruit cocktail (combined fruits, or melon balls, cantaloupe, watermelon, or honeydew)
Cantaloupe

Chilled slices of honeydew melon with lemon or lime
Grapefruit
Canapé: caviare, pâté de foie gras, anchovy, lobster, sardine

Food—Accessories:
Celery, plain or stuffed; olives—ripe or green or both; tiny gherkins; radishes, cut in "roses."

SECOND COURSE:

Choice of these:

Hot:
Chicken à la King
Lobster or crab or clam Newburgh
Broiled chicken or squab
Stuffed breast of guinea chicken
Soft shell crab
Patties: chicken, oyster, shrimp, crab, mushrooms, sweetbread, chicken and mushrooms (to be served in patty shells)
Creamed mushrooms, sweetbreads, oysters, chicken, sweetbreads and mushrooms, chicken and mushrooms (to be served in croustades, timbale cases, in paper cases, or on toast)
Croquettes: Chicken, lobster

Cold:
Salads: Chicken, lobster, alligator pear, fruit, crabmeat, shrimp
Aspics: Cold boned chicken in aspic, pâté de foie gras in aspic, crabmeat or lobster in aspic, celery salad in aspic
Creamed chicken mousse
Cold turkey or chicken or ham or lamb or tongue, or a combination of these "cold cuts." With potato salad, or celery salad, or vegetable salad, tomato jelly, or mint jelly (with cold lamb), aspic, or tomato surprise

Accompanying breads:
Small buttered finger rolls, cheese straws or cheese fingers, break sticks, Melba toast, croissants, toasted brioche, small biscuits

Sandwiches: Simple sandwiches to serve with salads, etc. Assorted sandwiches. Rolled sandwiches.

THE "SWEET" COURSE:

Ice cream, or frozen pudding or water ice (Served in a large mold or in individual molds)

Individual Molds: The individual molds may be in appropriate shapes: hearts, wedding-bells, cupids, bride-figure, groom-figure, four-leaf clover, slipper, horseshoes, calla lilies, lilies of the valley, and other suitable symbols

French ice cream, Neapolitan, vanilla, strawberry, cherry, may be served with a sauce of crushed fruit, strawberries, raspberries, pineapple, combined fruits, or caramel sauce, chocolate, butter scotch

With the ice cream:
Wedding cake, bride's cake, simple or elaborate frosted cake, or layer cake

or

Thin wafers, petite fours or other kinds of small assorted fancy cakes. (These small cakes may also be in the shape of hearts and other images appropriate for a wedding.) (May be iced with white or delicate pink frosting.)

Sweet-accessories:
Bonbons, mints—white or pink or chocolate covered; candied rose petals, pink, white, or other delicate shadings; salted or glacé nuts; glacé fruits; preserved ginger; frosted mint leaves

BEVERAGES

The useful rule of offering a choice between a hot drink and a cold drink should hold good in the plans for the beverages served at the wedding feast, no matter what type the refreshments are to be.

For serving hot drinks—coffee, tea, chocolate—large urns are most convenient and, placed at the ends of the buffet table, decoratively balance the table-picture. The caterer will supply these urns. The most convenient variety is the electric urn, of silver or nickel, provided with a regulated current that keeps the beverage at an even temperature but does not "boil" or "percolate" it. The coffee or chocolate is made in the kitchen and is poured into the containers, which are connected with an electric plug under or near the table. Bouillon may also be served in this way.

The cold drinks may be iced tea, coffee, chocolate, lemonade, orangeade, limeade, fruit lemonade or a fruit punch of some kind, served in a large bowl, provided with a ladle and surrounded by small, handled punch glasses or Apollinaris glasses.

Sometimes the urn for the hot drink is placed at one end of the buffet table, and the punch bowl at the other end. Or there may be a choice of hot drinks, one at each end of the table, and the punch bowl placed on a table in some convenient corner of the room.

As the base for the punch, iced tea may be used, or ginger ale, white or dark, or grape juice, white or purple. Simple combinations are white grape juice and ginger ale, orange juice or other fruit juices and ginger ale,—with an effort to "dress it up" by adding mint leaves and slices of oranges and lemon.

—Weddings: Modes, Manners and Customs

BEYOND SUMPTUOUS

IF ever a wedding breakfast was misnamed, it was the
one that graced this marriage [of Nellie Grant and
Algernon Sartoris]—though set beside the twenty-nine-
course dinners President Grant liked to give, it appeared
a mere snack. The seven courses (starting with soft crabs
on toast, and passing lightly through such dishes as croquettes of chicken with green peas, woodcocks and snipe,
before reaching the strawberries and cream, small fancy
cakes, punch *à la Romaine*, coffee and chocolate) were
served in the State Dining Room, at a table burdened
with pyramids of nougat and candy, 'Corbeils glaces a la
Jardiniere', 'Epigraphe la fleur, de Nelly Grant', and, at
the centre, a giant 'Bride cake' from which streamers
stretched to either end of the table and disappeared into
bowls of flowers bristling with flags wishing 'Success to
the President', 'Success to the Army', 'Success to the
Supreme Court' and 'Hail Columbia'. Each guest had a
piece of wedding cake, already boxed and tied with white
silk, and a menu printed on white satin beside his place.

—And the Bride Wore . . .

THE CAKE

THE BRIDE'S CAKE

THE bride's cake, usually a masterpiece of the confec-
tioner's art, is the central decoration of the bridal table.
(Or this cake may serve as the centerpiece of the buffet
table.) Often this cake rests on a stand decorated with
white roses and lilies-of-the-valley. Sometimes the cake is
made with an open space in the center and lilies-of-the-
valley or other small flowers are grouped in this center,
on a small standard that fits into the space. Or into this
space may be put a small bride-figure, dressed quaintly in

an exquisite lace wedding frock. Or a white satin base may fit into this central space and on this may stand together the bride-figure and the groom-figure, both dressed in quaint picturesque clothes of long ago. The bride's cake is usually a special white cake, handsomely iced, and is often ornamented with orange blossoms and inscribed in white with the initials of the bride and groom. The two or three initials of both names are used, not merely the initials of the surnames: C.F.N.—D.T.K.

On both sides of the bride's cake there are sometimes low bowls or cornucopias of white flowers, roses, sweet peas, orchids, or gardenias, or white lilacs.

The bride's cake usually contains the prophetic trinkets: a ring for the one to be married next, a cat for the old maid, dice for the luckiest, a wishbone for the one who will "achieve the heart's desire," a mitten for the bachelor, a dime or a new penny for the one destined to be wealthy, a four leaf clover or a horseshoe for the lucky one.

The bride cuts the first piece of the cake and perhaps the first few pieces.

There may also be favors—snappers of white and silver lace paper, a nosegay of waxed orange blossoms, figure place cards.

—Weddings: Modes, Manners and Customs

TWO CAKES

GRAND weddings in America were also occasionally graced by more than one cake, though here it was brought about by the great American tradition of 'his' and 'hers'. In October 1874, when the guests filed into the Chicago dining-room of Mr. Henry Hamilton Honoré, following the marriage of his daughter to young Colonel Frederick Grant (eldest son of President Ulysses S. Grant), they found at one end of the 14-foot table a 'Bride's Cake, decorated with natural flowers', and at the

other end a 'Groom's Cake decorated with natural
flowers'—and, as the lilac-coloured menus also informed
them, these were supplemented by stewed terrapin, escal-
loped oysters, sweetbread, turkey and oyster patties,
chicken and lobster salads, fillet of snipes 'in Paper cases',
boned quail and boned prairie chicken, both 'in jelly
form', plus a multitude of other cakes, ices, meringues,
wine jellies, fresh fruit, and fruit salad; and, to see it all
smoothly digested, tea, coffee, and that king of cham-
pagnes, Krug.

—And the Bride Wore . . .

BOXED SLICES

The custom of giving boxed slices of cake to guests was widespread.
It evolved from that of sending cake to invitees who could not attend
the wedding. Some hostesses adopted both customs, giving boxes to
guests at the reception and sending them to others.

IN addition to the bride's cake, there are usually pieces
of wedding cake, dark fruit cake, wrapped in wax paper
and then folded in tinfoil and packed in small white
boxes. These boxes are piled festively on a large tray near
the entrance, so that each guest may take one. Each box,
covered with plain or white moire paper, is tied with a
tiny, narrow white satin ribbon, and is embossed (in
silver) with the initials of the names of the bride and
groom. Sometimes these attractive boxes are used as
favors, placed at the places of the guests at a sit-down
breakfast.

If the wedding is small and the bride wishes to make
the boxes a bit more personal, she may buy the plain tiny
white boxes for the purpose (Dennison's), tie them with
the narrow white ribbon, and in the ribbon attach a spray
of orange blossoms, either fresh or waxed.

The thoughtful bride or her thoughtful mother will graciously remember to send by guests boxes of the wedding cake to friends who were not able to come to the wedding, or perhaps may mail the boxes, the following day, to friends who, because of illness or any other reason, were prevented from coming.

— *Weddings: Modes, Manners and Customs*

CHAPTER 10

The Honeymoon

A Gracious Exit

TRAVELING CLOTHES

AFTER the wedding reception and the feast, the bride and groom stay as long or as short a time as they wish or as their plans permit.

As the bride leaves the reception to change from her bridal finery to her traveling clothes, the bridesmaids gather near her—or at the foot of the stairs, if there are stairs—to see who can catch her bouquet. For the one who does catch it, there is the prophecy of being the next one to be married.

—*Weddings: Modes, Manners and Customs*

THE bride goes up to the room that has always been hers, followed by her mother, sisters and bridesmaids, who stay with her while she changes into her traveling clothes. A few minutes after the bride has gone upstairs,

the groom goes to the room reserved for him, and changes into the ordinary sack suit which the best man has taken there for him before the ceremony. He does *not* wear his top hat nor his wedding boutonnière. The groom's clothes should be "apparently" new, but need not actually be so. The bride's clothes, on the other hand, are always brand new—every article that she has on.

A bride necessarily chooses her going-away dress according to the journey she is to make. If she is starting off in an open motor, she wears a suitably small motor hat and a wrap of some sort over whatever dress (or suit) she chooses. If she is going on a train or boat, she wears a "traveling" dress, such as she would choose under ordinary circumstances. If she is going to a near-by hotel or a country house put at her disposal, she wears the sort of dress and hat suitable to town or country occasion. She should not dress as though about to join a circus parade or the ornaments on a Christmas tree, unless she wants to be stared at and commented upon in a way that no one of good breeding can endure.

The average bride and groom of good taste and feeling try to be as inconspicuous as possible. On one occasion, in order to hide the fact that they were "bride and groom," a young couple "went away" in their oldest clothes and were very much pleased with their cleverness, until, pulling out his handkerchief, the groom scattered rice all over the floor of the parlor car. The bride's lament after this was—"Why had she not worn her prettiest things?"

The groom, having changed his clothes, waits upstairs, in the hall generally, until the bride emerges from her room in her traveling clothes. All the ushers shake hands with them both. His immediate family, as well as hers, have gradually collected—any that are missing must unfailingly be sent for. The bride's mother gives her a last kiss, her bridesmaids hurry down-stairs to have plenty of rice ready and to tell everyone below as they descend

"They are coming!" A passage from the stairway and out of the front door, all the way to the motor, is left free between two rows of eager guests, their hands full of rice. Upon the waiting motor the ushers have tied everything they can lay their hands on in the way of white ribbons and shoes and slippers.

—Etiquette

PROPER GOOD-BYES

AT the end of the wedding there is one thing the bride must not forget. As soon as she is in her traveling dress, she must send a bridesmaid or someone out into the hall and ask her husband's parents to come and say good-by to her. If his parents have not themselves come upstairs to see their son, the bride must have them sent for at once!

It is very easy for a bride to forget this act of thoughtfulness and for a groom to overlook the fact that he cannot stop to kiss his mother good-by on his way out of the house, and many a mother seeing her son and new daughter rush past without even a glance from either of them, has returned home with an ache in her heart.

It sounds improbable, doesn't it? One naturally exclaims, "But how stupid of her, why didn't she go upstairs? Why didn't her son send for her?" Usually she does, or he does. But often the groom's parents are strangers; and if by temperament they are shy or retiring people they hesitate to go upstairs in an unknown house until they are invited to. So they wait, feeling sure that in good time they will be sent for. Meanwhile the bride "forgets" and it does not occur to the groom that unless he makes an effort while upstairs there will be no opportunity in the dash down to the carriage to recognize them — or anyone.

—Etiquette

— 177 —

She also, of course, said good-bye to her own parents and other family members, and did so before re-entering the crowd of guests waiting to say their farewells.

"THE MERRY DASH"

AT last the groom appears at the top of the stairs, a glimpse of the bride behind him. It surely is running the gauntlet! They seemingly count "one, two, three, go!" With shoulders hunched and collars held tight to their necks, they run through shrapnel of rice, down the stairs, out through the hall, down the outside steps, into the motor, slam the door, and are off!

The wedding guests stand out on the street or roadway looking after them for as long as a vestige can be seen— and then gradually disperse.

Occasionally young couples think it clever to slip out of the area-way, or over the roofs, or out of the cellar and across the garden. All this is supposed to be in order to avoid being deluged with rice and having labels of "newly wed" or large white bows and odd shoes and slippers tied to their luggage.

Most brides, however, agree with their guests that it is decidedly "spoil sport" to deprive a lot of friends (who have only their good luck at heart) of the perfectly legitimate enjoyment of throwing emblems of good luck after them. If one white slipper among those thrown after the motor lands right side up, on top of it, and stays there, greatest good fortune is sure to follow through life.

There was a time when the "going away carriage" was always furnished by the groom, and this is still the case if it is a hired conveyance, but nowadays when nearly everyone has a motor, the newly married couple—if they have no motor of their own—are sure to have one lent them by the family of one of them. Very often they have two motors and are met by a second car at an appointed place, into which they change after shaking themselves

free of rice. The white ribboned car returns to the house, as well as the decorated and labeled luggage, which was all empty—their real luggage having been bestowed safely by the best man that morning in their hotel or boat or train. Or, it may be that they choose a novel journey, for there is, of course, no regulation vehicle. They can go off in a limousine, a pony cart, a yacht, a canoe, on horseback or by airplane. Fancy alone limits the mode of travel, suggests the destination, or directs the etiquette of a honeymoon.

—Etiquette

But the guests must not overstep the bounds of good taste in their high spirits. It was not "good form to try to follow the bride and groom and play tricks on them," warned one etiquette guide:

> ANYTHING in the nature of fun between friends is permissible, and all the mischief and gaiety of the wedding-guest heart urges it to jokes. As long as the public does not share these jokes they are harmless enough; but to be made conspicuous and rather ridiculous in the eyes of outsiders is what no bride and groom enjoy and what their friends should stop short of inflicting upon them. Vulgar people may not always know when to stop. Gentlepeople are careful not to make their kind a laughing stock.

—Vogue's Book of Brides

HONEYMOON DESTINATIONS

As the nineteenth century began, it was not the custom in the United States for newlyweds to dash off right after or during the reception. Rather, in the days following the wedding, they received well-wishing friends, relatives, and acquaintances, sometimes with more parties.

But by the end of the century, the "wedding-tour" had become established, complete with fashionable destinations—that over the decades went in and out fashion.

> CUSTOMS in wedding trips have changed greatly with our habits of living and traveling. Twenty, even ten years ago, a bridal trip to some resort favored by honeymooners was regarded as an essential feature of the wedding— Niagara, Bermuda, Palm Beach, the Riviera if the groom's means permitted. To-day one couple may visit the Orient, and another go to Canada for the midwinter sports. They may vanish on board his yacht or hide in his hunting lodge or camp. Young people of more moderate means seek the seclusion of cottages in fishing camps or in quiet mountain resorts, or go directly to their new home; but unquestionably the sight-seeing wedding trip is no longer in favor.

> —*The Bride's Book of Etiquette*

CHAPTER 11

Wedding Gifts

ℰ

CHOOSING A GIFT

Not all types of gifts were appropriate for any acquaintance to make, and not all those invited to a wedding were obliged to send a gift. If one was given, it was always sent to the bride rather than the groom.

ANY person who is invited to a wedding may send a gift to the bride, but unwarrantable bestowals of presents upon her are an offence against delicacy. Only those who are on terms of unmistakable friendship are justified in sending bridal gifts. Those who violate this canon of refinement risk being thought intrusive or perhaps ostentatious. Such as bestow gifts should at least have what the Germans call a "Thee and Thou affiliation" with the recipient.

When the bride's family are in ordinarily comfortable circumstances at home and her future abode promises to be similarly appointed, Good Form does not permit those who are not especially near and dear, and certainly those who are mere calling acquaintances, to send her gifts of utility. The latter grade of presents is reserved for the two interested families. Silver, linen and house furnishings should not be sent as presents, except by kinsfolk,

baptismal sponsors, and life-long friends of the fathers and mothers of the two about to be united. Other or remote persons may present the bride with bric-a-brac, books, embroideries or odd little bits of antique silver that may properly be catalogued among *curios*.

By this plan, few or no duplicated gifts are purchased, because a combined family interest provides against this blunder.

— Weddings Formal and Informal

ℱℴ ℱℴ ℱℴ

DOES an invitation to a wedding call for a gift? This question must be considered from two angles, social and business or professional. Relatives and personal friends of the bride and the groom and of their families always send gifts. Acquaintances are governed by the wording of the invitation. Those who are invited to both church and reception send gifts. Those who are invited to the church only are not obligated to send a gift. An invitation to a reception following a private ceremony calls for a gift. Women who pride themselves on doing the kindly or gracious thing, often send the bride flowers on her wedding day, when they are invited to the church ceremony only.

Anyone who may not be able to attend the home wedding or reception because she is ill, in mourning, or traveling abroad, will send the usual gift, exactly as if she could be present.

Neither the clergyman who performs the ceremony nor the family physician is expected to send a wedding gift unless social relations exist between the two families.

Now for gifts sent by business acquaintances, who receive invitations to the church only. For example, an attorney and his wife may receive an invitation to the church wedding of the daughter of a client whose family they do not meet in a social way. If the husband wishes to

send a gift which represents his business friendship for the bride's father, it is sent to the bride in the name of himself and his wife. The same thing is done by a business man whose relations with the groom are friendly, though he may not know the bride or her family. The gift is sent to the bride with the joint card of the business man and his wife.

— The Bride's Book of Etiquette

It was not necessary to enclose a note with the gift.

THE card is sufficient. Congratulations and good wishes are offered at the wedding reception. When the gift is sent by a married woman who knows the couple socially, or who is merely selecting a present from her husband to a business friend, she incloses their joint card, "Mr. and Mrs. Russell Calder," or her husband's calling card and her own. If the gift is sent from out-of-town, or by anyone who cannot attend the reception, the phrase "with all good wishes" or something equally appropriate may be written across the card.

— The Bride's Book of Etiquette

MONOGRAMMING

EVERY piece of silver may safely be marked with the bride's family name, or with her cipher, as is all the linen she carries to her new home. Presents from the groom's family are given to the bride, and usually these are also marked with her maiden name. The latter custom is in questionable taste, except in such instances as requests to that effect are sent with unmarked gifts. Givers from the man's intimate friends have good form on their side if they

order silver, marked with the groom's cipher, or his name. But gifts from his immediate family, as was said, are intended as a welcome to his wife, and should bear her monogram, her initials, or her name.

— Weddings Formal and Informal

Later brides had a different view of the significance of their initials.

THE established custom calls for the marking of all linen and silver and gold plate, china and glassware, with the bride's maiden initials, thus: "M. W." for "Mary Walker," her maiden name, not "M. T." for "Mary Turner," her married name. This custom grew out of the fact that wedding gifts are the personal property of the bride. However, many modern girls who scorn old customs ask their friends to use the initials which will be theirs after marriage, thereby establishing their own family and its name. If you know her well, it is a good idea to consult the bride on this question. Thoughtful friends do not mark occasional silver articles, like candlesticks, carving sets or flower-holders because the bride may wish to exchange duplicates.

How soon are gifts sent? Usually two weeks or ten days before the date of the wedding, in order to give the bride the opportunity to acknowledge them.

— The Bride's Book of Etiquette

One etiquette guide went even further, proclaiming that

if marking is used at all the initials or the monogram should have the letter of the bride's married, rather than her maiden, surname. She is, presumably, going to live in her husband's house, under his name. To have the damask and linen for their joint housekeeping marked with her

own name only seems in bad taste. The choice between initials or monograms is hers to make.

—Vogue's Book of Brides

ACKNOWLEDGING THE GIFTS

THESE gifts may be sent at any time after her wedding invitations are out, and the earlier the better for her convenience, because it is rigid etiquette that she writes a note of thanks to each person who remembers her with a present. She is better satisfied if she completes this obligation before she leaves home. If the wedding journey is to be a long one, and gifts are late in arriving, it is especially inconvenient to fulfill this duty within a week after marriage, which is the outside limit of time custom allows for writing grateful responses to such delicate courtesies. Even the slightest gift is acknowledged, its value frequently being in the loyal and tender affection that prompted the sender to make, perhaps, a great sacrifice in presenting it. It is this latter idea of friendship and its expression that established a custom which prevails in families of fine feeling to remove the cards of those who send wedding presents before they are displayed.

As it is a usage, though not obligatory, that brides make no visits, or go to places of amusement, after cards are out for her marriage, the leisure thus provided by a kindly custom permits her to write notes and letters, it being improper to leave home as a wife, with any girlhood correspondents unanswered.

—Weddings Formal and Informal

❦ ❦ ❦

BEFORE starting on her wedding journey, [the bride] writes little notes of appreciation by hand. Wise brides list

each present as it arrives, with the date of receipt, the name of the sender or senders, and the shop from which it comes, the last in case she may wish to exchange the gift because of duplicates she may receive. She will save herself anxiety and the last-minute rush if she will acknowledge the gifts she receives each day before retiring at night.

What is the correct form for acknowledging wedding gifts?

> Dear Aunt Helen:
>
> Your wonderful gift made Jim and me so happy. We had hoped that some one would send us a samovar and candlesticks, but we hardly dared count on it. And now we have them with other Russian touches for our new home. You will come often to let me make tea for you, won't you, dear?
>
> > Affectionately,
> > Jane

Is it proper to exchange gifts? Yes, especially when duplicates of articles are received or when a gift is entirely inappropriate to the scale on which the newly married couple will live. It is better to exchange one of seven silver platters for a dainty breakfast service than to have no breakfast service!

—The Bride's Book of Etiquette

DISPLAYING THE GIFTS

In the nineteenth century, it was not considered "good form" to show the gifts to anyone but close relatives and friends. By 1930, that view was changing.

HERE is another question on which there is a wide difference of opinion. Families who pride themselves on their exclusiveness and good taste show wedding gifts to relatives and intimate friends only, a day or so before the wedding; but there is absolutely no objection to displaying the gifts for all who come to the reception. Usually a library, morning room, or bedroom from which the furniture has been removed is used for this purpose. Tables which can be rented from caterers or built with boards laid on wooden horses are ranged against the walls and through the center of the room, leaving aisles. The tables are covered with plain white cloths, damask, or fine sheeting, and the gifts are grouped in the best possible taste, silver on one table, glass and china on another, and linens on a third, all with a nice sense of color. There is much discussion also about the removal of cards from gifts. The punctilious remove them, but this is not a hard and fast rule.

—*The Bride's Book of Etiquette*

IS it customary to show presents the day of the wedding? Yes, it is usual but not essential. Many people do it but many do not. Showing the presents gives a certain amount of trouble: a room, or rooms, must be given up for the display of them, and a detective, or a watchman, employed to guard them.

—*Vogue's Book of Brides*

USEFUL AND TASTEFUL GIFTS

To start a proper household in polite society, the following items might be needed by the newlyweds.

Utensils, Glass and China*
For the Master's Table

GLASS

1	dozen water goblets	1	dozen claret glasses
1	dozen tumblers	1	dozen champagne glasses
1	dozen highball glasses	1	dozen sherry glasses
1	dozen cocktail glasses	1	dozen finger bowls with
1	dozen liqueur glasses		plates to match

CHINA

1	dozen teacups and saucers	1	dozen game and salad plates
1	dozen soup cups (for lunch only)	1	dozen dessert plates
1	dozen soup plates	4	vegetable dishes (2 covered)
1	dozen service or dinner plates	2	breakfast sets (Possibly tea and coffee sets
1	dozen entrée (or fish) plates		and meat platters, two or three)

For the Servants' Table

LINEN

4	tablecloths	4	dozen napkins

SILVER

2	dozen large-sized forks	1	dozen large-sized knives
1	dozen smaller-sized forks	1	dozen butter knives
2	dozen teaspoons	4	serving spoons, 1 ladle

*These lists may be reduced according to the size of the households. The necessities are named, but their number may be changed.

GLASS AND CHINA

1	dozen water tumblers	1	dozen meat plates
1	large glass pitcher	1	dozen salad or dessert
1	dozen soup plates		plates
2	meat platters	1	soup tureen
1	dozen cereal saucers	1	teapot
1	dozen cups and saucers	1	coffee pot
2	covered dishes (cereal)	1	sugar bowl
4	vegetable dishes	1	cream jug

For the Kitchen

KNIVES	SPOONS	FORKS
Bread	3 table	1 meat
Carving	1 mixing set	Pastry
2 paring	1 set measuring	Medium grater

MISCELLANEOUS

Can opener	Muffin flour sifter and tins
Spatula	Refrigerator set (glass)
Lemon squeezer	Double boilers
Tea strainer	Set mixing bowls
Pastry brush	Bread board
Funnel	Food chopper
Potato masher	Canister set
Round cake pans (2)	Bread box
Square cake pan	Cake crock
Pie tins (2)	Egg beater
Baking dishes (3)	Wooden cooking spoon

AT THE STOVE

Hotwater kettle	Soup pot
Teapot	Preserving kettle
Coffee pot	Ladle
Measuring cup	Strainer
Frying pan	Salt and pepper shakers
Six saucepans, with covers	Oven cloths
Cake turner	Clock

About the Sink

Dishpan	One agate pitcher
Wire drainer	Rubber scraper
Dishmop	Soap dish
Vegetable brush	Covered garbage pail
Sink strainer	Waste-paper basket

Miscellaneous Needs

Roasting pans (2)	Water pail
Step stool	Towel rack
Long-handled mop	Colander
Broom	Recipe file
Dustpan	Steel balls for scouring
Whisk broom	Paper napkins

—Vogue's Book of Brides

CHAPTER 12

The Trousseau

Our word *trousseau* is taken from Old French, in which it was a diminutive form of *trousse*, or bundle; thus, a trousseau is a "little bundle." Among the wealthier members of polite society, however, there was nothing at all little about a trousseau. It included linens as well as clothing for the new wife, and sometimes silver as well. In the nineteenth century a proper trousseau was meant to supply the couple for many years:

> IN these days of many needs and a still greater number of desires, it is no slight undertaking to provide a daughter's trousseau. This effort is not sufficiently understood by men in general, the detail of his own wardrobe previous to marriage being comparatively limited. A woman's outfit comprises not only her personal raiment, but house linen, of various grades, to serve from kitchen to garret. As a rule this supply is expected to be enough to last for at least a decade without additions, provided her fortune warrants thus much outlay from a bride's mother.
>
> — *Weddings Formal and Informal*

As the twentieth century progressed, fashions began to change so quickly that it became less practicable to try to plan for up to ten years hence. Even so, an "average" list for "a girl of background and family, marrying a young man of the same kind" was quite extensive, and for the "very rich" could be utterly lavish.

LINEN

For household linen the following average list is given, supposing the bride to have the means to entertain and to obtain real damask and good linen.

For the Table

1 very large tablecloth and 2 dozen napkins to match, damask.

2 medium tablecloths and 2 dozen napkins to match, damask.

6 smaller tablecloths (for everyday use) and 6 dozen napkins, damask.

2 lunch cloths, say, of Italian linen, and 2 dozen napkins to match,

(or)

2 lunch sets, centerpiece, and doilies, of lace or fine embroidery, 2 dozen small napkins to match.

6 traycloths for breakfast trays, 1 dozen napkins to match.

4 afternoon tea cloths and 4 dozen small tea napkins to match.

For the Pantry

2 dozen glass towels.

2 dozen dish towels.

6 roller towels.

2 dozen dust cloths.

4 chamois for cleaning silver.

4 polishing cloths.

For the Kitchen

6 roller towels.
1 dozen dish towels.
1 dozen glass towels.
1 dozen pot cloths.
1 dozen floor cloths.

For Each Master's Bed

4 pair of sheets, linen (and long enough to tuck in
    properly).
4 bolster cases, linen.
6 pillow cases, linen.
2 pairs of blankets (summer and winter).
2 counterpanes or bed covers.
1 eiderdown comforter.
2 mattress covers.

For Each Servant's Bed

3 pair of cotton sheets.
4 cotton pillow cases.
1 pair of blankets.
2 bedspreads.
2 mattress covers.
1 wool comforter.

For Each Master's Bathroom

1 dozen bath towels.
2 dozen hand towels.
1 dozen guest towels.
1 dozen wash cloths.
4 bath mats.

For the Servants' Bathroom

4 bath towels (each servant).
6 hand towels (each servant).
6 wash cloths (each servant).
2 bath mats.

This list would come to about one thousand or twelve hundred dollars and, marked, might easily reach fifteen hundred dollars or more. . . .

It can not be repeated too often that different ways of life and different surroundings must be taken into consideration when buying any sort of trousseau. Many girls, separated from their families and busily making their own way in the world, may be providing themselves with the wardrobe and household articles usually given by the bride's people. To them these lists will seem what an old acquaintance of ours calls "beyond the beyonds." To others, perhaps, they will seem inadequate. Let us hope the average reader will be satisfied, if not with the list as it stands, at least with the fact that it furnishes ideas to be followed or modified.

—Vogue's Book of Brides

ℱ℈ ℱ℈ ℱ℈

The Most Extravagant Trousseau
(one example)

THE most lavish trousseau imaginable for the daughter of the very rich might be supposed to comprise:

House Linen

One to six dozen finest quality embroidered or otherwise "trimmed" linen sheets with large embroidered monogram.

One to six dozen finest quality linen sheets, plain hemstitched, large monogram.

One to six dozen finest quality linen under-sheets, narrow hem and small monogram.

Two pillow cases and also one "little" pillow case (for small down pillow) to match each upper sheet.

One to two dozen blanket covers (these are of thin washable silk in white or in colors to match the rooms) edged with narrow lace and breadths put together with lace insertion.

Six to twelve blankets.

Three to twelve wool or down-filled quilts.

Two to ten dozen finest quality, extra large, face towels, with Venetian needlework or heavy hand-made lace insertion (or else embroidered at each end), and embroidered monogram.

Five to ten dozen finest quality hemstitched and monogrammed but otherwise plain, towels.

Five to ten dozen little hand towels to match the large ones.

One to two dozen very large bath towels, with embroidered monogram, either white or in color to match the border of towels.

Two to four dozen smaller towels to match.

One tablecloth, six or eight yards long, of finest but untrimmed damask with embroidered monogram on each side, or four corners. Three dozen dinner napkins to match. (Lace inserted and richly embroidered tablecloths of formal dinner size are not in the best taste.)

One tablecloth five to six yards long with two dozen dinner napkins to match.

One to four dozen damask tablecloths two and a half to three yards long, and one dozen dinner napkins to match each tablecloth. All tablecloths and napkins to have embroidered monogram or initials.

Two to six medium sized cut-work, mosaic or Italian lace-work tablecloths, with lunch napkins to match.

Two to six centerpieces, with doilies and lunch napkins to match.

Four to a dozen tea cloths, of filet lace or drawn work or Russian embroidery, with tiny napkins to match. Table pieces and tea-cloths have monograms if there is any plain linen where a monogram can be embroidered,

otherwise monograms or initials are put on the napkins only.

One or two dozen damask tablecloths, plain, with monogram, and a dozen napkins to match each.

In addition to the above, there are two to four dozen servants' sheets and pillow cases (cotton); six to twelve woolen blankets, six to twelve wool filled quilts, four to six dozen towels, and one or two dozen bath towels; six to twelve white damask (cotton or linen and cotton mixed) tablecloths and six to twelve dozen napkins, all marked with machine embroidery.

Two to six dozen kitchen and pantry towels and dishcloths complete the list.

—Etiquette

ℱℯ ℱℯ ℱℯ

SILVER

THE subject of the bride's silver is an interesting one and very much complicated by the fact that people who buy do not always know what is essential, and people who sell always try to persuade them to get a great many different sorts of implements. Many of these are unknown to smart service. Families who have always possessed silver are not easily persuaded to get all the modern contrivances, nor does an implement have to be named for its use before they know how to employ it. But newcomers to the silver game are impressed by the number of tabulated articles offered them. Many of these are unnecessary; among them round-bowled spoons for bouillon, sharp-nosed spoons for oranges, salad forks with the cutting tine, ice-cream fork-spoons, or spoon-forks, pastry forks (whatever they are), and the like. The best houses get on very well without any of these utensils, some of which may be added to the bride's chest if she should

want them, but none of which are in any way important. The not-to-be-ignored table silver is this: Four sorts of spoons; that is, teaspoons, dessert spoons, tablespoons, and after-dinner-coffee spoons. Three sorts of knives: first size, second size, and butter knives. Two sorts of forks: first and second size. (Perhaps oyster forks should be added.) Salt cellars, with their spoons, and pepper pots. And here are the reasons for this list. If a bride has, say, a dozen teaspoons they may be used for tea or coffee in the morning, for grapefruit or oranges, for eggs in the shell (though special gold-washed spoons are better, because they don't tarnish), for soup in cups or fruit cocktail at luncheon, for tea again at after-noon tea time. Now, if she has four teaspoons, four round-bowled bouillon spoons, and four orange spoons, she can only use them for the particular service for which they have been created—a service for which the teaspoons will do very well. The dessert spoon may be used for cereals in the morning as well as for dessert. Oddly enough, dessert spoons are not much in favour with the general public, but they are used, invariably, by society everywhere. They are set, with the second-sized fork, on every dessert plate, for both lunch and dinner. The large-sized spoon is used for soup at dinner (which is, for this evening meal, *always* served in soup plates), and it is also used, with a large fork, for serving purposes. After-dinner-coffee spoons are only for after-dinner coffee.

At smart tables the second-sized knife may be used for anything that is to be cut at breakfast or luncheon—unless there is a course of meat demanding a larger implement at the latter meal. This is also true of the second-sized fork, which serves for any food but the heavier sort of meat.

At dinner the second-sized knife and fork will do for fish, for an entrée, for the game and salad course—for everything, in fact, but the roast or meat course. The butter knife is the same at all meals. Fish knives and forks may be added to the silver list later, as may orange

spoons, or anything else desired, but the real essentials might be considered covered in the following list.

Spoons

18 teaspoons for various uses.
12 dessert spoons.
18 large spoons for soup and serving.
12 after-dinner-coffee spoons.
12 ladles.
 4 salt spoons.

Knives

12 large knives.
18 second-sized knives.
12 butter knives.

Forks

18 large forks for meat and serving.
24 second-sized forks, for fish, entrée, salad, and
     dessert.
12 oyster forks (could also be used for lemon
     with tea).

Silver trays are useful—the flat kind that really hold dishes or after-dinner coffee cups, not those foolish ones with a slanting edge that hold nothing.

Gravy boats or sauce boats in silver are also very useful.

Sugar tongs, sugar sifters, and a tea strainer are really necessary.

Four salt cellars and four pepper pots at least should be bought.

If anyone is disposed to give a bride a tea set of silver, an after-dinner coffee pot in silver, and a hot-water kettle in silver, the bride should be more than content, but she should stand out for several silver trays, and, if possible, a silver meat platter.

Of course, tea or coffee can be served as well in china, and there's an idea among young housekeepers that it is difficult to keep silver clean, which, with modern methods, is hardly the case. This list is for those who not only love the sheen of this lovely metal, but can afford about twelve hundred dollars' worth.

No doubt, there are more articles mentioned than are needed by many brides, and perhaps fewer than some of the specially petted ones will receive, but as an average it is not out of the way and may help some young woman toward a decision.

It would be quite possible to curtail this list, and taking the total number of people whom a young couple in modest circumstances would be likely to seat at table as four—or eight, with bridge in prospect—it might be reduced as follows:

Spoons

12 teaspoons for various uses.
8 dessert spoons.
12 large spoons (4 for serving).
8 after-dinner-coffee spoons.
1 ladle.
2 salt spoons.

Knives

8 large knives.
16 second-sized knives.
8 butter knives.

Forks

12 large forks (4 for serving).
24 second-sized forks (for three courses) (16, if one set can be washed between courses).
8 oyster forks.

Second-sized forks, it may be pointed out again, at a dinner party must be three times the number of other forks. They are set for fish or entrée, for the salad course, and with the dessert spoon on the dessert plate. It is possible, however, although a disagreeable necessity, to wash them after the first course and slip them into place on the dessert plates, which are always ready on the sideboard.

Plated ware is often bought before silver can be afforded and comes in many beautiful patterns. It can always be used, even if silver supersedes it, in the summer country places of people who do not carry their silver with them everywhere. Some of the designs in plated ware are as classically lovely as any in silver. Of course, the difference in price is enormous. For such a list as the last given the silver pieces might cost about five hundred dollars where the same amount of plate might cost from about eighty to one hundred dollars.

—Vogue's Book of Brides

CLOTHING

Average Summer Costume Wardrobe

1   country coat, tweed, for all occasions.
1   town ensemble (coat and dress to match).
2   figured crêpe de Chine or chiffon dresses.
2   two-piece crêpe de Chine dresses in light colours.
3   simple day dresses in wash silk or linen (for sports and country).
4   hats (three suitable for sports and country wear and one for formal wear).
4   simple evening dresses.
1   simple evening coat.
2   dressing gowns (cool, one a little plainer than the other).
1   summer raincoat.
2   parasols (one a sun umbrella).

Winter Costume Wardrobe

1   fur coat and (probably)1 fur neck piece, if
    in fashion.
1   cloth coat, possibly fur trimmed, for town (this
    should be selected to go with all dresses, for
    ensemble effect).
1   cloth dress.
2   crêpe de Chine dresses.
1   country ensemble (three-piece, with extra top
    coat, also for town wear in bad weather).
1   country hat (also good for bad weather in town).
3   town hats (one a little more formal than
    the others).
1   evening coat (chosen with regard to each
    evening dress).
1   very formal evening dress.
2   dresses for dancing.
1   dress for dinner, with extra jacket (this can be
    used with other dresses for restaurant
    and theatre).
2   tea gowns, or 1 tea gown and 1 set of dinner
    pajamas and coat.
2   dressing gowns (warm, one a little plainer than
    the other).
1   raincoat.   1   umbrella.   1   evening bag.
2   bags, at least, to match outdoor costumes.

Underwear and Accessories for Both Summer and Winter

3   slips.   6   brassieres.
6   daytime underwear sets.   6   nightgowns.
6   evening underwear sets.
4   athletic sets (for sports clothes).
4   pair of wool and lisle stockings.
6   pair of stockings (daytime colour).
6   pair of stockings for evening wear.
1   pair of street shoes (morning).
2   pair for afternoon.

2	pair of country shoes (one pair of these for active sports wear).
3	pair of evening slippers (one pair to match best dress, two pair to wear with any dress).
8	pair of tan or beige suède gloves for town wear.
6	pair of chamois or wash gloves for country wear.
3	dozen handkerchiefs, day and evening.

—Vogue's Book of Brides

❦ ❦ ❦

How many dresses can a bride wear? It all depends—is she to be in a big city for the winter season, or at a watering place for the summer? Is she going to travel, or live quietly in the country? It is foolish to get more "outside" clothes than she has immediate use for; fashions change too radically. The most extravagant list for a bride who is to "go out" continually in New York or Newport, would perhaps include a dozen evening dresses, two or three evening wraps, of varying weights. For town there would be from two to four street costumes, a fur coat, another long coat, a dozen hats and from four to ten house dresses. In this day of weekends in the country, no trousseau, no matter how town-bred the bride, is complete without one or two "country" coats, of fur, leather or woolen materials; several homespun, tweed or tricot suits or dresses; skirts with shirt-waists and sweaters in endless variety; low or flat heeled shoes; woolen or woolen and silk mixture stockings; and sport hats.

If the season is to be spent "out of town"—even in Newport or Palm Beach—the most extravagant bride will find little use for any but country clothes, a very few frocks for Sunday, and possibly a lot of evening dresses. Of course, if she expects to run to town a great deal for lunch, or if she is to travel, she chooses her clothes accordingly.

So much for the outer things. On the subject of the under things, which being of first importance are saved for the last, one can dip into any of the women's magazines devoted to fashion and fashionables, and understand at first sight that the furnishings which may be put upon the person of one young female would require a catalogue as long and as varied as a seedsman's. An extravagant trousseau contains every article illustrated—and more besides—in quality never illustrated—and by the dozens! But it must not for a moment be supposed that every fashionable bride has a trousseau like this—especially the household linen which requires an outlay possible only to parents who are very rich and also very indulgent.

—Etiquette

CHAPTER 13

Remarriage

In theory the general rules for a second wedding were the same whether the woman or the man was the one remarrying (or both were). However, since so much more detail was involved in the bride's costuming, whether for a first or later marriage, than in the groom's, and the bride's choice of dress set the tone for everything in the wedding, much more attention was paid to advising widows and divorcees than to widowers and divorced men. Some doyennes of etiquette, unfortunately, saw this as an opportunity to dwell on their disapproval of divorce and especially of women who divorced (without consideration of the causes). Others, however, recognized divorce, and remarriage, as a fact of social life and seemed content to help their readers make the best of it. Views toward widows were similarly conflicted, and this showed in contradictory customs about their dress in particular.

CONSIDERATIONS FOR MEN

What a man needed to know was easily summed up as follows:

> WHEN either bride or groom has been married before,
> or when they have passed middle age, or when the family

of either is in mourning, the wedding may be celebrated quietly in church or at home as early as 10:30 A.M., and the bridal couple will leave at once on their wedding journey. . . .

When a man marries a second time, he is governed by the same customs that prevailed at his first wedding, but he rarely gives a farewell dinner to his men friends.

—The Bride's Book of Etiquette

CONSIDERATIONS FOR WOMEN

DRESS AND CEREMONY

In the late nineteenth century,

ON both sides of the Atlantic there were stern rules for widows who chose to remarry and these forbad all thought of white. John Cordy Jeaffreson put the English point of view like this: 'A widow at her re-marriage, provokes no criticism by wearing a silk of sober or fuscous tint. It is indeed held by some critics that any colour, with the single exception of black, is more appropriate than white for a gentlewoman's robe of state at her second marriage, and that she has no more right to the dress of virginal brides than to the decoration of wreath and veil, or the services of bridesmaids.' Mrs. Earle illustrated the same maxim with a story of one of her own 'kinswomen ' who was married first at 17, widowed within a few weeks, and then married again ten years later. 'She wore "coming out bride" a silver gray satin gown, and a gray pelisse of uncut velvet with a silken stripe; this was lined with cherry-coloured satin and trimmed with marabout plumes. Her bonnet was of shirred gray velvet with natural gray feathers and cherry-coloured face trimmings of very full ruches of ribbon loops . . . a charming costume, but she was exceedingly unhappy because, having been a widow, she could not in etiquette appear in a white bonnet and feathers and veil. And she felt that coming a stranger to her new home it was so unfortunate to appear in a gray bonnet; that it made her seem like an old woman, and was "so conspicuous".'

—And the Bride Wore . . .

However, another etiquette advisor of the period viewed widow remarriage quite differently:

THERE was once a stateliness, if not a severity in the formalities attending marriages of widows, as if in rebuke to them for wedding again, but all that, very properly, has fallen into disuse.

It is possible that an influencing sense of justice to woman brought about an abandonment of such austerities, since a widower re-marries with as much gayety as he would assume if he were a bachelor. Etiquette allows widows as many bridesmaids, maids of honor, and pages as she chooses to invite, also all the sumptuousness of spectacular accessories, if she prefers such pomps. Custom, that always inflexible mistress of social affairs, denies her a veil and orange blossoms, but she wears a robe of white, if it is becoming to her, and her age does not make its appearance incongruous.

As a rule, however, she chooses a shade or two away from white, preferring rose, salmon, violet, or ivory, not for any poetic reason, but because such a change is an advantage to her own color.

Of course, a woman who is clever in grades of attire, familiar with social fitness and the best standards of taste cannot possibly make her appearance whimsical, at her marriage. A pretence of youth, after youth has taken leave of a woman, simply intensifies personal evidence of age,

and is a pathetic spectacle. This is less often noticeable in a woman's dress, however, than in her manners.

Fashion which is social law, no longer disapproves of attire, white raiment, jewels and flowers for the advanced matron, whether she is bride, wife or widow, unless she is unmistakably aged.

— Weddings Formal and Informal

Similarly, a few decades later:

THERE was a time, but it is ended, when widows could not wear white when re-marrying, because custom disallowed it. White is now the robe of all brides, if they prefer it, but veils are approved only at first marriages. Orange blossoms are no longer *de rigueur* at weddings of maidens, but are worn or carried, if desired. They were never good form for brides who were widows, on account of their legendary significance.

— Weddings: Modes, Manners and Customs

And yet:

THE marriage of a widow is the same as that of a maid except that she cannot wear white or orange blossoms, which are emblems of virginity, nor does she have bridesmaids. Usually a widow chooses a very quiet wedding, but there is no reason why she should not have a "big wedding" if she cares to, except that somber ushers and a bride in traveling dress, or at best a light afternoon one with a hat, does not make an effective processional — unless she is beautiful enough to compensate for all that is missing.

A wedding in very best taste for a widow would be a ceremony in a small church or chapel, a few flowers or

palms in the chancel the only decoration, and two to four ushers. There are no ribboned-off seats, as only very intimate friends are asked. The bride wears an afternoon street dress and hat. Her dress for a church ceremony should be more conventional than if she were married at home, where she could wear a semi-evening gown and substitute a headdress for a hat. She could even wear a veil if it is colored and does not suggest the bridal white one.

A celebrated beauty wore for her second wedding in her own house, a dress of gold brocade, with a Russian court headdress and a veil of yellow tulle down the back. Another wore a dress of gray and a Dutch cap of silver lace, and had her little girl in quaint cap and long dress, to match her own, as maid of honor.

A widow has never more than one attendant and most often none. There may be a sit-down breakfast afterwards, or the simplest afternoon tea; in any case, the breakfast is, if possible, at the bride's own house, and the bridal pair may either stay where they are and have their guests take leave of them, or themselves drive away afterwards.

Very intimate friends send presents for a second marriage but general acquaintances are never expected to.

—Etiquette

ᔮᕽ ᔮᕽ ᔮᕽ

THE bride at her second marriage usually chooses to have a simple, quiet wedding, to take place in a chapel of the church, or in the drawing-room of the bride or her mother. Sometimes she has no attendant and sometimes one attendant, rarely more. Only members of the two families and a few intimate friends are invited to the ceremony.

At her second marriage, the bride (even if she is very young) does not wear a white dress or a bridal veil or

orange blossoms; nor does she carry a bouquet of white flowers.

The discriminating woman, if her second marriage is in church, will wear either a beautiful afternoon frock, rich-looking perhaps or sophisticated in line, with a hat, or she may wear a traveling suit. A lace dress, often of beige lace over a pastel-shaded slip, is an appropriate costume.

After the ceremony, as simple or elaborate a breakfast or tea as the bride wishes to plan, is served.

— Weddings: Modes, Manners and Customs

INVITATIONS AND ANNOUNCEMENTS

It was most correct for the parents or other relatives of the bride to send out invitations and announcements for a divorced or widowed woman, especially if she was young.

FORM OF FORMAL ANNOUNCEMENT
FOR DIVORCEE OR WIDOW
(To be engraved in Script or Roman Letters)

Mr. and Mrs. Stephen Orris

have the honour to announce

the marriage of their daughter

Gertrude May James

to

Mr. William Vane Nesbit

on Saturday, the fifteenth of November

one thousand nine hundred and twenty-eight

at Old Trinity Church

New York

FORM OF FORMAL ANNOUNCEMENT
BY BRIDE AND GROOM
(To be engraved in Script or Roman Letters)

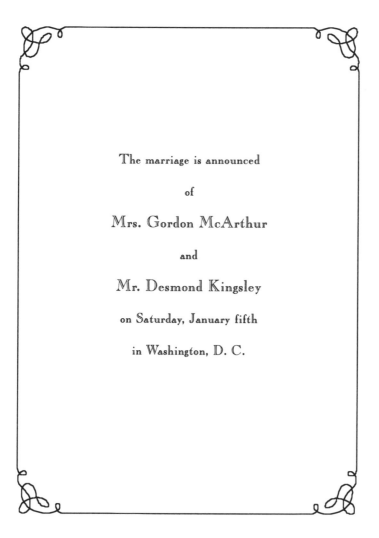

The marriage is announced

of

Mrs. Gordon McArthur

and

Mr. Desmond Kingsley

on Saturday, January fifth

in Washington, D. C.

If a woman has any relation living who can announce her marriage, that relation should do it. If she has none and still wishes to announce it, she might do it in this way, speaking of herself in the third person and therefore using her title, whether married or single. The procedure is, however, most unusual and would be unsuitable for the young. . . .

In cases where parents are sending out invitations to the wedding of a divorced daughter the last name need not be mentioned either, unless people prefer to do so. But in public notices, such as are sent to the newspapers, the last name of the daughter by a first marriage or of the divorced daughter would be given. Those are notices to the world at large—a world not necessarily concerned with private affairs until told of them in print. The social world is supposed to be better informed. With a widow the last name is generally used. Neither divorcée nor widow would be spoken of as "Mrs."

—Vogue's Book of Brides

CHAPTER 14

Married Life

CONDITIONS OF MARRIED HAPPINESS

From the wedding, it was expected (as now perhaps it is more often hoped), a couple embarked on a lifetime together. In the equivalent of the many advice books of today for those seeking happiness, one guide of yesteryear ventured the following "conditions" for a good marriage over the decades.

1. No view of marriage is satisfactory that does not regard it as a tender and respectful friendship, "embellished," as a brilliant Frenchman adds, "by an incomparable mutual possession." We feel inclined to emphasise this view as of the greatest practical importance in perpetuating married happiness. The want of tenderness, either by the adoption of an over-bearing manner, which never reaches cruelty even in intention, or by what is still more characteristic of northern nations, the silence or sparse expression of love, even when it is felt, has a wearing effect upon its objects. A sentiment so tender as married love ought to be manifested. Much can be said against "gushing" and untimely demonstrations of marital affection, but undemonstrative conduct is not without its

dangers. We have a terrible warning in the case of a famous teacher of his age, who learned too late, when his beloved one was taken away, how deeply he had failed in sufficiently expressing by word and act the feeling with which he regarded her.

2. Not less to be combated is the tendency for all the courtesies of the sweet-heart period to diminish, and sometimes to disappear, from married life. There should not be allowed to enter into the homestead any—even good natured—disrespectfulness in language or manner towards any of its members. More depends upon the observance of this caution than many people realise. The only lady whom many a man habitually treats uncivilly, is his own wife; and the only gentleman for whom many a lady will take no pains to be pleasant and attractive, is her own husband.

3. Want of unity of aim is another prolific source of domestic failure. This has many sides, and enters into economics, child-training, the cultivation of good neighbourly relationships, the maintenance of a satisfactory footing with the relatives of both sides of the house, the relativity of work to relaxation, the quality and allotment of joint pleasures, and the formation of new friendships. Pitfalls in abundance attend every one of these illustrations of the want of oneness in aim. Unless there is mutual confidence as regards personal and household expenditure; unless each parent supports the other in the exaction of discipline among their offspring during the period of childhood, and a few years beyond it; unless each is complaisant towards neighbours and family connexions; unless they "see eye to eye" upon the ratio to be maintained between the serious and recreative portions of existence, and can co-operate in united tours, visits, expeditions and the like, and unless new alliances are the subject of mutual assent, troubles will grow in unlimited profusion "Union is strength" is an old adage; but in married life it is more: it is peace and comfort.

4. Hitherto we have spoken only of union in the practical concerns of wedded life, but no thoughtful person will undervalue the conviction "that any real and permanent union of human beings must rest on a sufficient harmony between them in respect of the three portions of our spiritual nature—feeling, intelligence, and what is properly called character; and this harmony should be more complete in proportion as the union is to be intimate and profound" (Ingram). Profession of the same religious faith becomes, therefore, an important item in family concord.

—Things a Gentleman Would Like To Know

ANNIVERSARIES

The following anniversaries were generally recognized:

First:	Cotton	*Fifteenth:*	Crystal
Second:	Paper	*Twentieth:*	China
Third:	Leather	*Twenty-fifth:*	Silver
Fourth:	Silk	*Thirtieth:*	Pearl
Fifth:	Wood	*Thirty-fifth:*	Coral
Sixth:	Iron	*Fortieth:*	Ruby
Seventh:	Wool	*Forty-fifth:*	Sapphire
Eighth:	Bronze	*Fiftieth:*	Gold
Ninth:	Pottery	*Fifty-fifth:*	Emerald
Tenth:	Tin	*Seventy-fifth:*	Diamond
Twelfth:	Silk and Linen		

—Weddings: Modes, Manners and Customs

It may seem overly optimistic to account for a seventy-fifth wedding anniversary, and it's uncertain whether any of polite society actually achieved that landmark. However, a sixty-fifth anniversary was recorded, although one had to search rather far afield to find it.

A "Crown-Diamond" Wedding.
Sixty-Fifth Anniversary.

WITH iron weddings, as humorously described by Max
Adeler, and with silvern, golden, and diamantine weddings, as celebrated in Continental countries, the British
public is tolerably familiar, at least by hearsay. So far as
we know, however, a "Crown-Diamond" wedding, such
as was celebrated a few days ago at Maibuell, in the
island of Alsen [in Denmark], is a ceremony altogether
without precedent in matrimonial annals. Having completed their sixty-fifth year of conjugal bliss, Claus
Jacobsen and his venerable spouse, both of the above-
named place, were solemnly blessed by the parson of their
parish, in the presence of a crowded congregation, and
went, for the fifth time in their long wedded lives,
through the form of mutual troth-plighting before the
altar at which they had for the first time been united a
few days before the battle of Waterloo was fought. The
united ages of this crown-diamantine couple amount to
one hundred and seventy-eight years; and Claus
Jacobsen, despite his ninety winters, still works daily in
his carpenter's shop at the handicraft by which he has
unintermittently earned a living for himself and his family
throughout more than two-thirds of a century.

— *Wedding Etiquette and Usages of Polite Society*

More commonly, one might celebrate a fifth, tenth, fifteenth,
twenty-fifth, or fiftieth year of marriage, often with a party. The following would have been appropriate invitations for each occasion:

Wooden Wedding.

THE invitations are engraved on wood, or imitation, in form:

1810.   1815.

Mr. & Mrs. Rip Van Winkle,

At Home,

Wednesday evening, June seventh, at eight o'clock.

10 Broadway.

No gifts received.

Tin Wedding.

Engraved on paper in imitation of tin, in form:

1810.   1820.

Mr. & Mrs. Rip Van Winkle,

At Home,

Tuesday evening, June seventh, at eight o'clock.

45 Chambers Street.

No gifts received.

Crystal Wedding.

The invitations are engraved on crystallized cards, in form:

1810.   1825.

Mr. & Mrs. Rip Van Winkle

request the pleasure of your company

at their Fifteenth Wedding Anniversary,

Wednesday evening, June seventh, at eight o'clock.

475 Broadway.

No gifts received.

Silver Wedding.

The invitations are engraved in silver or in black with the dates in silver, in form:

1810.   1835.

MONOGRAM
R V W. S V.

Mr. and Mrs. Rip Van Winkle

At Home

Friday evening, February fifth,

from eight until twelve o'clock

Kaatskills, N.Y.

No presents.

Golden Wedding.

The invitations are engraved and printed on Wedding Note Sheets, in gold. Form:

1810.   1860.

MONOGRAM

RVW. SV.

Mr. Rip Van Winkle   Miss Sally Vedder

Mr. and Mrs. Rip Van Winkle

request the pleasure of your company

to celebrate the Fiftieth Anniversary

of their wedding,

Wednesday afternoon, September twenty-first,

at two o'clock.

Irvington, N.Y.

No presents.

— Wedding Etiquette and Usages of Polite Society

Celebrations varied according to the couple's station and means.

Wooden Wedding.

MR. AND MRS. T. CHESLEY RICHARDSON, 55 East Fifty-sixth street, celebrated their "wooden wedding" on Tuesday evening, January 27. Many unique and appropriate presents were received. Cedar tubs, and bowls, and pails, and baskets filled with flowers, transformed the room into a blooming garden. There were elaborately carved tables with embroidered coverings, cabinets of oak and ebony, wall brackets of artistic design, beside *bric-a-brac* stands, paintings on wood, paintings framed in wood, beautifully worked wooden plaques, boxes of beautiful woods for various uses, etc., etc. One of the most noticeable of the presents was a large bog-oak dog, superbly carved, holding a pearl tray as a card receiver. Some seventy or eighty intimate friends were present, many of whom witnessed the marriage ceremony of Mr. and Mrs. Richardson.

Silver Wedding.

MR. CHARLES CROCKER, one of the wealthiest men of California, the land of colossal fortunes, celebrated his silver wedding at his residence, California and Taylor streets, San Francisco, on the twenty-seventh of November. The bride and groom received their guests in the drawing-room under a floral arch. The toilet of the hostess was remarkable for its elegance and appropriateness. She was attired in a heavy white satin, brocaded with silver, *princesse* style. The skirt was vandyke, with heavy silver tissue knife pleatings, and covered with silver net-work and white satin bands, the whole being trimmed with *duchesse* lace. Her hair was dressed in puffs, and she wore an elegant set of brilliants, which set off the toilet exquisitely. Her jewelry consisted of a necklace of six

strings of diamonds, the centre one valued at $8,000. The ear-rings were long, and each contained three large diamonds. Miss Crocker, the only daughter, a young lady just budding into womanhood, was attired in a plain *ecru* silk. Her only ornaments were turquoise jewelry. At ten o'clock the rooms were crowded with ladies and gentlemen. The display of toilettes was unusually rich and brilliant. Nearly every dress in the room represented a small fortune, and diamonds flashed from the neck, ears and head of nearly every lady present. The guests had been interdicted from sending any present, but this did not prevent Mr. Crocker from making his wife a present of an elegant case of silver, made in New York.

❧ ❧ ❧

MR. AND MRS. JESSE SELIGMAN celebrated their silver wedding last Saturday evening, at Delmonico's. There were nearly five hundred guests, who were received by the bridal couple under a canopy of flowers, attended by their daughters, the Misses Alice, Emma, and Madeline, who were dressed as bridesmaids. Three beehives, made of flowers, represented the absent sons of Mr. and Mrs. Seligman.

Golden Wedding.

DR. JAMES CRAIK, pastor of Christ Church, Louisville, Kentucky, and wife celebrated their golden wedding last Wednesday. One of the guests from a distance was Mrs. Virginia Smith, of Wheeling, Va., a bridesmaid of Mrs. Craik fifty years ago. It was pleasing, says the *Courier Journal*, to see the number of old folks who came out to do homage to the half-century bride. Mrs. Craik carried an exquisite bouquet of roses and orange flowers, which was presented to her by a friend, while Dr. Craik had pinned to the lapel of his coat a spray of rich glossy holly, chaste and unique. The children and grandchildren

were all present, except Rev. Charles Craik, who is in
Switzerland; Mary Craik David, who is in Texas, and
Alexander Casseday, who is in the far West. At two
o'clock the rectors of Calvary and Grace churches, with
Dr. Norton, assistant rector of Christ Church, together
with the choir of Christ Church and a few friends, came
into the parlors, where Dr. and Mrs. Craik met and wel-
comed them. Mr. Joe Craik then brought his babe; an
altar was improvised, and the beloved old father and
grandfather took the infant in his arms and blessed it and
baptized it in the name of the Holy Trinity, after which
a beautiful and impressive service as held, the clergy,
in their robes, officiating in turn, Dr. Craik making
the prayer of thanksgiving. A member of the vestry then
read a testimonial of affection and trust to Dr. Craik,
reminding him that just ten years ago was the twenty-fifth
anniversary of his pastorate over Christ Church, speaking
of their abiding love and faith, and their hopes for many
years to come. Dr. Craik tried to respond, but wet eyes
and quivering tones attended more than words, and a
voice from the people said softly the words of benedic-
tion, "Well done thou good and faithful servant." Guests
now streamed in from everywhere, until there seemed
hardly room for the ovation. The parlors were most beautifully and appropriately decorated. There was a great
marriage bell, made of wheat fully ripe. There were
shocks of corn. There were autumn leaves of purest gold
color, yet with light touches of green nestling about their
heart. There was a great horseshoe made of Maréchal
Niel and orange flowers, with the number fifty in its
centre, made of white rose-buds and holly leaves. There
were the dates 1829 on one side of the wall and 1879 on
the other, bound together with an unbroken chain of
golden straw. There were festoons of cedar and evergreen
linking the old and the new. There was a great anchor of
tuberoses and rose-buds resting on a crown. There was a
great basket of autumn fruits, winey grapes and ripe
peaches and golden bananas. There were flowers in every

form, typical stars of light, horns of plenty with golden roses falling out, and baskets of trailing vines. The lace curtains were looped back with rich red leaves, and an illumined motto, dressed in ferns, bore the words, "Their children shall rise up and call them blessed." The dining-room was also dressed, and a handsome table spread by Christ Church invited all to partake of its cheer. The wedding cake bore the monogram of James Craik and Juliet Shrewsbury, in golden letters, with the dates 1829 and 1879. Christ Church also sent a band of music, which was placed on the lawn and gave out the sweetest music on the air. The lawn itself seemed to have caught the festive spirit, for a great sumac tree held up its ruddy torch, while beeches and maples took on the faintest tint of gold.

— *Wedding Etiquette and Usages of Polite Society*

Works Cited

And the Bride Wore . . . The Story of the White Wedding, Ann Monsarrat. Initial letters by Elisabeth Trimby, (New York: Dodd, Mead & Co., 1974).

The Bride's Book of Etiquette, Anna Steese (Sausser) Richardson, (New York, London: Harper & brothers, 1930).

Etiquette: The Blue Book of Social Usage, Emily Post, (New York: Funk & Wagnalls Company, 1923).

Things a Gentleman Would Like to Know Concerning Etiquette, Health and Exercise, Michael Brett, (London: Hutchinson & Company, Inc., 1970).

Vogue's Book of Brides, (Garden City, New York: Doubleday, Doran & Company, 1929).

Wedding Album: Customs and Lore Through the Ages, Alice Lea Mast Tasman; picture editor, Laurie Platt Winfrey, (New York: Walker, 1982).

Wedding Etiquette and Usages of Polite Society, George D. Carroll, (New York: Dempsey & Carroll, 1879).

Wedding Toasts and Traditions: Sample Toasts and the Origins of Customs, Mark Ishee, (Brentwood, TN: J M Productions, 1986).

Weddings Formal and Informal, Abby Buchanan Longstreet, (New York: Frederick A. Stokes Company, 1891).

Weddings: Modes, Manners and Customs, Mrs. John Alexander King, (New York: Delineator, 1928).

Wedding Books from Hippocrene . . .

Polish Wedding Customs and Traditions

Sophie Hodorowicz Knab

From best-selling author, Sophie Hodorowicz Knab, comes this unique planning guide for Americans who want to organize and celebrate a Polish-style wedding. Sections titled Engagement, Bridal Flowers, Wedding Clothes, Ceremony, Reception and even Baby Names, will assist the bride-and groom-to-be through every step of the wedding process. Special tips on "How to Draw from the Past" at the end of each chapter provide helpful suggestions on how to incorporate Polish tradition into the modern wedding, to make it a truly distinctive and unforgettable event. Photographs and illustrations throughout.

Sophie Hodorowicz Knab is author of *Polish Herbs, Flowers & Folk Medicine* and *Polish Customs, Traditions & Folklore*. She writes a column for the *Polish American Journal* and resides in Grand Island, N.Y.

196 pages • 6 X 9 • photos/illustrations • 0-7818-0530-9 • W • $19.95hc • (641)

Under the Wedding Canopy: Love and Marriage in Judaism

David C. and Esther R. Gross

This comprehensive book delves into the wide range of marriage customs, ceremonies, traditions and practices that have become part of the Jewish heritage for nearly four thousand years.

"An ideal gift for couples . . . practical, full of useful information."
> —*The Forward*

"Jewish wedding customs from around the world . . . advice on how to create a happy marriage."
> —*American Jewish World*

"A portrait of Jewish marriage that is unfailingly positive and unabashedly traditional."
> —*Na'amat*

243 pages • 5½ X 8½ • 0-7818-0481-7 • W • $22.50hc • (596)

Treasury of Wedding Poems, Quotations & Short Stories

illustrated by Rosemary Fox

Looking for the perfect poem or quote for a wedding day toast? This treasury of over 100 classic poems, quotations and short stories from around the world, entirely on the subject of weddings, is sure to contain it! With 30 charming illustrations, the lovely gift edition is also a perfect wedding present. The collection contains selections from over 50 authors, including A.A. Milne, Gerard Manley Hopkins, Goethe, Anne Bradstreet, Anton Chekhov, Judah Halevi, Bella Akhmadulina and Unnur Benediksdottir.

150 pages • 6 X 9 • 30 illustrations • 0-7818-0636-4 • $17.50hc • (729)

All prices subject to change. **To purchase Hippocrene Books** contact your local bookstore, call (718) 454-2366, or write to: HIPPOCRENE BOOKS, 171 Madison Avenue, New York, NY 10016. Please enclose check or money order, adding $5.00 shipping (UPS) for the first book and $.50 for each additional book.